VERSES AND VISIONS:

The Road Ahead

John T. Eber, Sr.

Managing Editor

A publication of

Eber & Wein Publishing

Pennsylvania

Foreword

As I read through many of your comments and personal statements, I couldn't help but notice one word that was regularly mentioned: Outlet. Where many of you indicated how poetry provides an outlet for creativity and honing in to improve one's writing ability, others claim it is an outlet to escape pain, sorrow, or everyday stressors. And even a small number confess how writing a poem is a personal cleansing process with nothing but a purely cathartic purpose. But whether indicative of a creative outlet or a therapeutic one, I found the imagination, motivation, passion, and raw emotion behind the verses in this collection truly remarkable. The nice thing about such an outlet is that it encourages repressed feelings and emotions to surface and even instigates new approaches to past events— for example, what once triggered painful, melancholy feelings might later welcome witty, lighthearted humor after a period of reflection. Or just the opposite may happen when experiencing tragic loss or the death of a loved one. Although poetry shouldn't always be limited to just personal experiences, such experiences shared in this volume are quite moving, and we are honored to publish them. I can't say how many times I've been told that poets draw a great deal of inspiration from reading other poets' work and how even a secondhand witness of their experiences can be powerful and influential. I hope this is the case for you and that you find all of the poems here worthwhile. As a teacher, I always stressed to my students that there is nothing more refreshing, invigorating, or educational than for a poet to read another poet's work. Poetry is a craft to be shared and you have ultimately provided us and each other with small glimpses of the world as it exists through your eyes. Continue to be free and let go!

John Eber Sr.

Memories

I found a flower pressed
    Between the pages of a book.
Its old and faded colors
    Had a withered wrinkled look.

Yet a fragrance faintly lingered
    As an echo of the spring,
Of blooming meadows basking
    In a warm and sunny place.

Antiquated memories
    In a warm familiar room
But when I brought it to my face
    To sniff the frail bloom,

The pale petals caught a gust
    And fluttered to the floor.
They crumbled into dust
    And were no more.

A. O. Sanan'aho
Columbus, NE

1

To Whom It May Concern

Hope that when you read this
you learn something.
I might not make sense or even
leave you in suspense
but if you're a little smart
you will keep it in your heart
Sit down, relax, and open your mind
from your very first word…
to everything you've done that was absurd
When you became an ugly beast…
And your mother always tried to defeat.
The times your mother tried to explain…
And all you did was complain.
Didn't even give it a moment of thought…
That it was your mother you had struck.
Tears falling like when rain pours down…
Just went ahead and pushed her around.
Ask yourself what went wrong?
Did you want to belong?
Maybe your friends gave you a love so profound.
Why are you just standing there…
With such a sad stare?
Did you ever stop to think that
Your life would one day stink?
Did you ever once tell her "I love You"?
Look around, where are your friends
Now that you're so down?
I hope you one day regret it
And never forget it…this happened
Because you let it…can't take
Anything back…well it's really too late for that!

Irene Medina
Fontana, CA

2

Loving Hands

My children when you were young, I held your hands in mine
To guide you past the evil in this world I knew you'd learn in time
I could not be with you always
but my hands in prayer would pray
that our Heavenly Father would guide you
and get you through the day.
Now that you are older and do not need my guiding hands
I'll pray you'll always be in my heart
and someday you'll understand.
Let us all remember there also were wonderful hands
That loved us so
They were nailed to a cross—still clinging to life; did not want to let go.
Those hands are still there to guide us as mine are too
To help each loved one get past each day
and make it easier to get through.
Now my dear family as we get older
You don't need my hands much more
But you know I need your hands now
to help us balance and walk and get us safely through each door.
Thank your Heavenly Father each day
For hands wrinkled-smooth, callused or pierced with nails
Reach out always to help someone
Helping someone with our hands, love never failed.

Lenore Brinkerhoff
Provo, UT

Road Called Identity

I am a flower,
Bright and unique.
I am a bee
Loud and annoying.
I am a weed,
Stubborn, but free.
All of this, is all of me.
I am free from the clutches
Of tree branches.
I spiral anywhere
My heart pleases.
No one can cut me down,
I am strong.
I belong,
Where I belong.
The road I take
Is my identity.
My identity
I will keep.
No one treads,
No one creeps,
On the road,
My identity sleeps.

Claudia Atkinson
Bensalem, PA

A Sunset Sublime

Tonight I captured the sunset
Behind the mountain it met.
It dropped behind a cloud's brim
With gold around the rim.

The sun bowed down to rest
Beneath its bed in the west.
It filled my soul with rapture,
Its grandeur I did capture.

May my life at the close of day,
Be as supreme I pray.
As I pass from this present life,
With all its toil and strife.

May a crown of glory await me there,
As bright as the sky is rare.
To dwell with the Lord on high,
In that glorious home in the sky.

Jeanne Pewitt
Asheboro, NC

A Warning

Don't lean on me
so strongly,
if you want our love
to survive.
I am not as strong
as I appear to be.
I am fragile and
perhaps even dangerous
like a mirror glass
that can be broken
and cut the skin,
or the apparently peacefulness
of a lake that can kill
if you don't know how to swim.
If you want to be with me
I offer you my hand
to walk together
through the path of life.
You will see
what you want to see.
I will do the same
without expectations
from you.
We will be together
by the moments
that we will spend together
never by the years
or by the word: FOREVER.

Andy Rivera
Elmhurst, NY

Fact Faith Feeling

Fact, faith, and feeling,
Were walking on a wall.
Feeling looked down,
Then the trio took a fall.

You see, the Christian life,
Must first be based on fact.
You find that in the word of God
That's the only place its at.

Second comes the faith,
When you believe all that is true
About the savior Jesus,
And what he's done for you.

Third will come the feeling,
But to feeling do not cleave.
I'll admit it's nice,
But feeling will also leave.

I'm sure you remember Peter,
God's chosen fisherman.
It was when he looked down,
That he went for a swim.

But we have a sure foundation,
It's Christ He is our all.
Unless you keep your eyes on Him,'
You will have a fall.

Norm Cutler
Pensacola, FL

It Never Really Meant Much

It never really meant much, when someone would smile at me.
It never really meant much, in this world my eyes had seen.

But then I heard your story, and the pain you made me feel.
And my heart grew to love you, in warm compassion that's all too real.

The absence of a loved one, and the toll that has taken place.
Simple whispers of their name, bring tears of sorrow and heartbreak.

Now the moon in all its glory, is no longer a sight to see.
It is dark and ever so lonely, as something is lost inside me.

I can't help but wonder, how in spite the sadness that I feel.
How the daily world around me, continues in motion as if it was real.

The sun still rises each morning, and the stars still twinkle at night.
But my heart sees no beauty, as it's been taken from my sight.

I never really knew you, the one who left this place.
But I feel your presence within me, in the warmth of a loving embrace.

As you are my kindred spirit "eternal in love" is what I believe.
And even after your passing, a world of beauty I will see.
Because, since my life before you…

It never really meant much, when someone would smile at me.
It never really meant much in this world my eyes had seen.

Marie Brightman
St. George, UT

8

Apple Pickin' Day

I was anticipating their arrival
But it was only the rain that was arriving
Then a burst of joy came through the front door
I heard those children's voices that I so adore
Isaiah proclaimed how could a little rain deter
It was Abigail who shouted grandma we're here
There was Machaira Micaela Grace
With a great big smile upon her face
As she stood there oh so shy
There was a tear that came to my eye
I watched the apples of God's eye
As they climbed up toward the sky
As the day passed oh what a sight
The sun now shown bright
And of that brother how he has grown
He has taken on a New Life of his own
Being just like his earthly father he is busy acting like his Heavenly
Father
The girls painted rainbows with colors just right
As the beauty of the full day turned unto night
I collect all my hugs and kisses and give a big sigh
as the girls and I make silly grins and waves good-bye
As they traveled down the long driveway
I realize that this is the way that we survive

Kathleen J. Eggers
Elk River, MN

9

Loving the Enemy

In this world
There are two types of girls
Ones that are beautiful
And those that make you hurl

Was there such a thing
As a beauty in between
There was the one
My beautiful queen

Sadly we were separated
And away from our wish
To share the thing we wanted
An everlasting kiss

We would sneak out at night
And look at the starry sky
Wishing to be together
Just you and I

Soon our parents found out
We were to be killed right away
But we both ran from home
To share longer and brighter days

Earl Collins
Ozone Park, NY

Growing Up

I watch as you do your own thing.
I pray you can face what it may bring.
You're not a child anymore . . . I can't tell you how to live—
But look at your life, what a mess!
You think you know it all, well if your way is right
Why are you in such pain?
There are many things that you don't know.
I've been here longer, had more time to grow!
You say growing up is hard to do.
It isn't easy for anyone; I'm still growing too—
The way you are going about it is all wrong!
All of those drugs and guns won't make you strong!
Can't you see there is no easy way, growing up is what life is all about.
The ground you are walking on is weak and will make you fall.
You say your friends and drugs will see you through life.
Their brains are weak and drugs will make you rot!
Do you have one friend who would care if you had food or clothes to wear?
The time will come when you will see,
Your friends are not what you thought they would be!

Wendy Horwath
New Bern, NC

Gabriel Life's Joy

Words cannot express how I feel today,
on this your graduation day.
My special gift from God above to ease my troubled way.
Gabriel you are unlike any other.
A light that shines for all to see,
with your caring loving way.
How proud I am, how dear you are to me.
I wish life's very best, with happiness abound,
in all things great and small.
The Lord grant you health and happiness but,
most of all good friends to share the way.
May he guide and protect you,
and be with you at the start of each new day.
You will never realize how much you mean to me.
I love you more than life itself.
I am proud to say you are my son each and every day!
With love on this your special graduation day!

Grabrielle Velasquez
Clovis, NM

Our Promise

You'll always have your space
I'll take my own pace

Within our family past,
Present and future,
We will always take time
To nurture

If you ever hear a dove
Singing "Coo" "Coo" "Coo"
It's just me saying
I love you

Because doves stay
Together forever
Our love will never
Die for each other.

Linda McCormick
Park City, IL

Pondering Eva

Last evening,
A silky milkweed seed brushed across a newborn's wispy hair,
drifted away again in the breeze,
moved toward the sunset,
like a spark spiraling upward from a fire into the night sky.
This morning,
while hearing of my great aunt Eva's passing,
dew disappeared into thin air from my front yard.
Just now,
I found a single strand of her white hair,
clinging to the shoulder of the sweater she left behind.
And suddenly,
I remembered the dream I had last night,
of her sitting among family, smiling.

Lori Nunnally
Loveland, CO

A Child's Mental Anguish

She trembles as her vacant eyes well up with tears.

The sun dances in pools of deep reflections from her exquisite sky-blue
eyes
that are old beyond their years.

A child tortured day in day out by mindless messages of words, and
thoughts floating across her brain like a parade of demons.

Days pass with no sadness, no smiles, just in perceptual state of limbo.

Others hear voices penalizing them for uncommitted sins or forcing them
into heinous acts.

Some have highs of happiness and lows of depression so severe they
can't
function.

These are the faces of the millions, who suffer silently within this hidden,
shameful disease society refuses to acknowledge, "mental illness."

Marcia J. Brown
West Hills, CA

To My Children

Conceived out of love
Humbled and honored just to be your Mother
Instantly smitten when I first
Looked into those eyes
Devoted to you forever
Rising to the occasion
Even when you were wrong
Nurtured with caring and concern, never
wanting to leave you to the injustices of
this world without my blanket of love.

Norma T. Chuilli
Plymouth, MA

My Grandpa

As nice as leeches
Down at the beaches
My Grandpa is grumpy
His stomach is lumpy

My Grandpa's the best
He knows I just jest
When I call him a grump
And suggest that he's plump

Austin Pompano
Meriden, CT

In the Looking Glass

Who is this young woman?
Where is she from?
Why does she exist?

There is something so familiar…
Twenty-one years ago, another so liked her.
The same shape,
    Same mannerisms,
    Same fears, same wonder, same love.
And now, twenty-one years later,
You, her shadow, carry on the traits
    And habits that she unknowingly gave.
Yes, you show pride in who you are…
    her pride.
You should love whence you came…
    her love.
You show determination to exist in you own right,
    also hers.
Child, you came from love, and you exist to
    give love.
Now realize the positive soul in you
    is only borrowed from the young
    woman who gave you life twenty-one
    years ago…

Tammy Green
Memphis, TN

17

A Touch of History

He came from England
to this land which was
trying to be free.

His name was Thomas Paine
and the pamphlet that
he wrote was read
by all the people
from Georgia to Maine

In 1776 the title Common Sense
made a great important stir
and because of Thomas Paine
We took seriously the claim
"We have it in our power to
begin the world again."

Corinne Kiluk
Pittsfield, MA

Winter's Joy

Lacey snowflakes spiraling
   down my window.

Welcoming, whistling tea kettle
   on my stove.

Bright sparkles complete
   the rainbow.

Before the frost compliments
   the snow.

Carolers greet the year's ending,
   in a ray of hope,
Santa's sleigh is bending
   down our wintry slope.

Sylvia Smith
Liverpool, NY

Night-Time

The sun sinks slowly in the west,
And twilight dons her cloak and vest.
The silence whispers where steps have trod,
"Come back, come back, the night is young."
The whispering breezes run to and fro,
As fireflies spread their eerie glow.
The golden moon shines bright as day,
To light the way for the fairys' play.

The stars descend from their hidden throne,
To shine until the night is gone.
The wise old owl begins to stir,
From his sleep in the forest's tallest fir.
The animals peep from their hidden homes,
And venture forth to play and roam.
The glistening dew on the grass so green,
Shines like diamonds for a fairy queen!
The crickets strike up their merry band,
And send you off to slumber land.
The bull frog croaks his throaty tune,
In sharp contrast to the golden moon.
And as the night approaches dawn,
The velvet darkness is all gone!

Barbara L. Williams
Rossville, GA

A Christmas Poem

This Christmas I'll have everything.
A promise of today and hope for spring.
Eyes to see beauty like a baby's bright smile.
Ears that hear laughter from a small happy child.
Plenty of food on the table to eat.
A roof over my head and shoes for my feet.
A family so close that we feel each others pain.
The green of the grass after a big healthy rain.
A faith in my God that can't be taken away.
A country at peace and a freedom to pray.
This Christmas my gifts won't be under the tree
in a gift wrapped package with the name tag for me.
This Christmas I'll have everything.
The joy of tomorrow. The birth of a king.

Jonnie L. Taylor
Polk City, FL

Sounds of War

Is that the sound of a far off war
Or the wind that batters at my door
Is it the lightning that flashes and dies
Or the thunder that rumbles across the skies

Is it the rain that is lashing the trees
Or just a storm out on the open seas
Is it the cold from my window sill
Or could be a dog from a nearby hill

It could be my feelings in the night
Or it could be just the horrible fright
It could be memories of the dead
Or it could be something that was said

It could be I'm dreaming of my home
Or it could be that I'm dead and all alone
The sun through my window now I see
I'm alive! I'm home! and I'm still free!

Margaret R. Finely
Oroville, WA

I come from a long list of poets, some published and some not. I have been a member of the Fraternal Order of Eagles for twenty-nine years. I have written poetry for the last four Washington State Presidents and for one Grand Madam President. Something about writing really relaxes me, I love to write and let my mind wonder. "Sounds of War" came to me just like most of my poems, when I'm in bed. My mind goes over and over the same thing till I get up and go to my computer to write it down, then I can go back to bed.

Dark Cloud Arise

A dark cloud has arose
Causing family cries.
A cloud that has erupt our lives,
causing pain with nothing to gain.
Wondering when pain will end,
remembering the date it all began.
Not proud of the dark cloud,
my heart cries out loud
go away. Go away dark cloud
hope you're not here to stay.
You're here when it shines and here
when it rains.
Dark cloud, dark cloud stop causing
this pain. You're driving this family insane.
Bring back the family years
without all the tears
Dark cloud, dark cloud

Debra A. Salter
Bronx, NY

My Goddess, Then Now and Forever

Mother, I should've spent more time listening
instead of worrying about shining and glistening
with diamonds, gold, and rubies
Neglecting the real jewels being bestowed upon me
with facts of life, morals, and structure
and realizing who really cares about you
plus the ins and outs of this unpredictable place
to prevent the slap in the face
such as hurt, loneliness and deceit
and nonetheless how to stand firm on two feet
tools which you beat me over the head with
which are my most cherished and loved gift
but at times I can be completely hard-headed
instead of applying what has been embedded
I wasted time and didn't realize
All along I held the key and grand prize
in doing so I ended up in my hell
caged away for years in jail
which deprived me from my precious Ila Mae
who took me under the wing from the first day
My goddess you are an outstanding mother
and the glory received can never come from another
so continue to look after me no matter the weather
and I'll continue to miss you then, now and forever

Raymond K. Legette
Brooklyn, NY

Just Imagine

A world without vines, there would be no grapes
A world without stalks, there would be no corn
A world without stems, there would be no wheat
A world without leaves, there would be no trees
A world without oil, there would be no cars
A world without rails, there would be no trains
A world without rain, there would be no harvest.
A world without rivers, where would the rain go
A world without water, there would be no seas
A world without water, what would we drink
A world without limits, there would be no space crafts
A world without knowledge, there would be no jets
A world without briars, there would be no blackberries
A world without sun, it would always be night
A world without bees, there would be no honey
A world without love, I wouldn't have met you
A world without sin, there would be no deaths
A world without sorrow would be paradise
A world without God we wouldn't be here
A world without Christ where would we go

Eugene Seal
Treadway, TN

Cabin

You are built like a door frame.
Wrapped delicately in alcoholic flannel
I can smell you from here.
You are built like a windowpane
That you fogged up yourself.
Do you think anyone will notice?
Your voice is the blustery day
That turns umbrellas inside out
Your tense your barometric pressure
And did anyone sigh?
You are built straight and true.
Notched wood that will keep out the winter
And when I tried to move into you
I saw.
You are Lincoln logs.

Ellen Steves
Seattle, WA

Your Passionate Kiss

Dew-dappled rose petals caress me
as a heady feeling engulfs me.
Bittersweet honey trickles on my lips
and I feel a tepid breeze.

Pitter-pattering rain-drops send jars through my body
that tease my yearning heart.
Soft ocean waves tickle my face
As two drums beat the same rhythm…
…a rhythm of LOVE

Stacey Dorish
Myrtle Beach, SC

Untitled

In time when she knew not
How man needs others.
She existed alone and observed
How man fulfilled others.
Eternity thrives
She now knows
On others.

Mary K. Coleman
Annapolis, MD

60 Years Ago

A white house atop a hill
A creaking swing, a cowbell
An apple tree, a stream that flows
But that was 60 years ago

A black and white dog that romped all day
Noisy children, kids at play
An old black mule, a garden and hoe
But that was 60 years ago
That wild wilderness oh so free
Towering plants, birds and bees
Unpolluted air, a dog named Mo
But that was 60 years ago

A factory now is in its place
Where the white house used to be
And all that remain
Are the memories

Susan L. Martin
Spring Hope, NC

Freedom

This nation is free,
But it came with a price.
When this land our fathers did see,
They did not think thrice.

They suffered and died.
They fought and sweated,
So this land could be freed,
Yet we take it for granted.

Let's not waste it.
Let's not take advantage.
We have many a critic,
Who will take it from our age.

We must work and fight,
Maybe fight and die
To keep freedom insight,
So on freedom we may rely.

Eric Cooper
Grennwood, IN

Untitled

Fish have to swim
Birds were meant to fly
Life has its meaning
on earth
Not up in the sky
What is this meaning
of life you may ask
To figure it out that
is your task
To sit in the silence and
not in the gloom
To be all that you can be
when you walk into
a room
Every word that
you speak
Every sound that
you utter
Is a drop in the bucket
that says this is you

Joan Rausch
Palm Springs, CA

Frozen in Time

Time stopped,
but the clock tick-tocked.
I see nothing move,
but children still snooze.

Church bells ding,
I hear someone sing.
Oh, what a beautiful sound,
tis' better than a heart's pound.

A little girl, dressed as a fairy,
carries a basket with one single berry.
She sings of love, hope, and passion,
of pencils, pens, and fashion.

I'll never know who that little girl was,
or even what she plays, sings, or does.
I'll only know of the little fairy,
who carried a basket with one single berry.

Brandy McDaniel
Jacksonville, AR

31

Trust

Oh how could one live
Through a single day
Without God leading
Each step of the way
Only He knows and understands
The anxieties and pressures
The world demands
Only to Him can you go
In times of despair
And know He will help
With just one little prayer
So when life looks real dark
And there is no one to care
Just run to him
As he's always there
And say, "Lord take my hand
tell me what to do,
because I put all my trust
in you"

Josepha P. Mitchell
Auburn, WA

Tantalize

In water, feigning fulfillment and nearness,
with nourishment that's teasing and pendulous,
a king whose misdeeds are dark and irreverent,
is deposed from a Lydian throne,
to endure the god's punishment,
where eternity is decreed to atone.

Now Tantalus, surrounded by temptation,
is the tortured prisoner of deprivation,
and PELOP, victimized by filicide and egoism,
enrages ZEUS and Olympian magic banishes death,
giving Poseidon the love of PELOP'S breath,
with beauty surpassing an earlier blossom.

Carl Pollack
Brooklyn, NY

The Beach

I go to the beach, it's so
quiet and serene and if you've
been there before, you know what
I mean. I let my mind wander
and take its time to unwind.
You don't hear the ringing of phones and the bustle of trains.
You just hear the waves crashing
on the rocks all around as your
thoughts are scattered, it's the
waves making the sound. The
beach makes my mind wander,
and I sort out my thoughts; it
makes you feel free and also alive,
it makes your mind clear and puts
things in perspective. Thank God
for the beach and it is an elective.
Take my advice and you'll see what
I mean. What a wonderful life
with a beach in the scene.

Donna Cavanaugh
Portland, CT

Last Leaf

Look at me, a crumpled leaf
Ragtag and bedraggled—
Hanging loosely on the tree
Tossed about by every breeze

Other leaves from my same season
Silently let loose and fly—
Falling
Twirling
Fluttering
Whirling
Ever downward
in
the
sky

My fellow leaf, my buddy
Slipped off the branch with ease
Drifted downward
Floated freely
Came to rest on earth beneath

Why do I hang here alone—
Dry and spent and solitaire
Swept in every breeze that blows
But still reluctant to let go?

Nancy Morgan
Whittier, CA

35

Grow

When it is dark, and not yet day
The Lord did come to me and say,
Tho it be dark, I give you light
Read my word, and grow in might.
For all is there, for all to see
Each word in my book was breathed by me.
You're only human, do what you can
teach them the difference, between GOD and man.
Many have no view of what's in store
Yet it was all written long before.
Man does think only of himself.
Yet in my word, lies all his wealth.
See and I will leave you never
Follow and you will live forever.

Poet Of The Lord
Santa Maria, CA

Lying in the Gutter

He lay there in the gutter.
A sorry sight to see,
I pondered and thought,
"But for fate lies me."
He rummaged through the garbage.
His shoes were all in shred.
He is a nobody,
a derelict who begs.
Yet he is a human being,
part of all mankind.
His image haunts me.
Engraved in my mind,
with his long uncombed hair,
his clothes a sight to see,
I close my eyes,
but for fate goes me.

Hilda Preston
Torrance, CA

Social Graces

Hello, how are you?
Me?
Everything is fine...really it is.

> *Heart throbs*
> *Head pounds*
> *Eyes swollen and sore.*

What's that?
No, don't worry about me—
Things couldn't be better...really.

> *Endless pain*
> *Sleepless nights*
> *Body shakes all over.*

What's wrong?
Nothing, nothing at all.
It's all good...really it is.

> *No voice*
> *No choice*
> *Hopelessly alone*

Good-bye, nice to see you.
See you later...

> *No, not really.*

Eileen M. Page
Scituate, MA

Raining Gold

Atop our mountain
The sky enchantingly blue
No clouds about
Began to suddenly
Rain gold
It was a magnificent sight
The quiet yet quick winds took the golden leaves
And fluttered them about
Far above our heads as they continued to
Rain gold
Shedding their beauty and wonderment about
Our troubled
Yet hopeful
World

Diane Whalen
Chicago, IL

Our Son, Sleepy

Almost six years to create
Almost nine months to wait
Only fifteen minutes to sweat
Eight days for grandma to fret
When I arrived I let out a wail
I'm here! Feeling fine now that I'm
Out of that jail
Now, I'd much rather sleep
And I'll be good temporarily
Besides the folks in maternity
Have been pretty nice to me
It's too much to ask after I leave
And I don't expect my dad to believe
That when he takes me home
And puts me in the nursery
That I'll blissfully slumber
And be as good as good can be
No! I'll kick up a fuss
And let out a squall
And personally see to it
That dad gets no rest at all

Harry Rowe
St. Clr Shores, MI

Porcelain Doll

That stylish, thoughtful porcelain doll,
So sweet and beloved—
Would rather live each day in your arms
Than sit upon a shelf collecting dust.

For although some rainy day she may fall,
And shatter her face a bit,
She will remember how it was
To romp and dance and sing.

And if, perhaps, she does forget;
The scars in the mirror will remind her
How she got that way—
the day you took her out to play.

Erin L. Cashin
Cohoes, NY

Sea

Sea, like a
Ghostly woman past
I left forever yesterday,
When I near the place you are,
I contrive to see you;
Arrange to touch you.
Then I am lost.
Timeless, you fill the limits of my world;
Provide passage for my phantom soul.
Eternities later
I become blasé from excess beauty;
Jaded, sense-dulled from your liquidness
And the revelations of frequent entries;
Tired from love-fear.
So I turn away.
In the corner of my eye,
As I do,
You become again
Boundless, untamed, worldwide,
Sweeping, haunting, beckoning,
Unknown as before.

Robert Kennedy
Santa Maria, CA

To Those Who Love me

As I sit and contemplate
On my dull and dreary fate
Tendrils of my mind wander
Back to those that I've grown fonder
Back in time back in space
Where I no longer have a place
To memories filled with joy
A happy girl, a mischievous boy
And childhood years all rush in
Joy, I had back then.
As the image slowly darkens
Leaving me in my despair
Memories of loved ones hearken
Those I loved and those that cared
Bored of what I say
Of people loving you everyday
Knowing that whatever you do
Someone cares what happens to you.
Knowing that you'll leave a space
When time comes to leave this place
Dear God above I only pray
That I may always live this way

Sherry Foster
Lawton, OK

The Voice

I can hear the thunder
And the rain beating down
Then it all stops
And I don't hear a sound.

As I lay here in the silence
As if I had no choice
Deep inside my head
I hear that nagging voice.

That voice knows me all too well
From inside and out
My soul can hear it yell
I wish it wouldn't shout!

It knows how I'm really feeling
It knows exactly what I am thinking
And why I feel so stressed.

It knows right from wrong
But little does it care about the good and the bad
I try to ignore its manipulations
It rages deeper when I'm mad.

It tries with all its screams
To keep me from the light
It haunts me in my dreams
And corrupts me more each and every night.

Sonia Stewart
Lawrenceville, GA

Abstract Realities

Who will explain these abstract realities,
so difficult to comprehend
Will you or I or perhaps Plato or Einstein
Often they say—the answers are carried on the wind
Yet the message is sometimes hard to understand
As if in a foreign tongue
A single sentence in a secret code, repeated like an S.O.S.
How soothing the persistence—Siren like, dream like, a trance
Dazed, confused, haunted by subconscious questions—I cry
Oh! These abstract realities, so hard to ponder,
Who will explain them?

Gary L. Isaacs
Connersville, IN

Death of a Soldier

He always gave us the best he could,
I know now what he understood.
I took his hand and held it fast
I knew that soon his pain would pass.
He whispered something
I could not hear,
I knew the end was very near.
I drew his head up to my breast
Gave him a place of final rest.
We're still alive, but he is free.
I've wondered if that's
The way it has to be.

Leslie Steen
Escondido, CA

45

Dewdrop Seconds

The baby sees all and more
And that's what we should dive towards
Precipitate your perception!
Unchain your day and find your infant's eye
I am an intricate and you are a duplicate
Do not waste the sky
We each receive a new horizon daily, but it differs
All the energy bottles itself for us
Blind monsters with perfect eyes stifle us always
Just regress back to genius and then discover what infinity entails
Help me through and I'll help you too
Release me and I'll find my way home
Or take me away, far above this plateau
All these things I don't just say, I wish to know
It's hard enough to drag let alone tow
I've found the eye but lost the supply
It happens in a dewdrop second and the next thing you know
Your body will ripple
Don't panic, it's simple
Oceans of spilled milk are smooth sailing seas
When you find your way up off your knees
Infinity entails an infant's eye in a dewdrop second

Jason Leppert
New Enterprise, PA

Grand Garden

Sitting in a garden at
a small table for two,
lilac and roses filled
the air with perfume.
We sat at the table
small cups in our
hands, green tea and
biscuits, with raspberry
jam.

The frogs were jumping
as if in play.
Birds were singing
a melody of song.
You looked at me
and said, I'm happy
to be with you this
beautiful day. This
beautiful morn.

Jean Cast
Huntington, NY

I started writing at the age of ten and had my first poem published at that time. When I was 11, I wrote and directed a play for the girl scout troops that I belonged to. I had my poems published in the women's North Shore newspaper. Several of my poems have been published by the National Library of Poetry. My father was also a writer. I have two children and a grandson. I was inspired to write this poem while sitting in my friend's garden, filled with wildflowers and roses.

The Real Me

I wish I could see the real me,
    speaking true thoughts inside of me.
Projecting a radiant and sincere smile
    locked somewhere deep inside.

When will I speak true words that I really mean?
Or continue to say the acceptable thing.
Some expressions don't express what I really feel
    there is so much more inside to give.

Is it wrong to think differently from others?
To accept the wrongness of sisters and brothers.
Should truth and honesty stay buried inside
    while greed and selfishness stand with pride?

Each day I become more perplexed
    when closer to the truth I get.
People want you to conform and be quiet,
    and continue to keep your true feelings inside.

Inside or Outside, I must be free
    to truly express the "Real Me."
Whether it be love or hatred that unfolds,
    the "Real Me" must be exposed.

Mattie Millikin
Detroit, MI

Scoliosis

When it gets hard for you to bend,
      Please, spend more time with me,
We will be wild,
We will be free.
      Two candle flames flickering
Draw oxygen into our lungs to survive,
And collapse,
      When we are finally out of breath,
Then you can talk and I will be silent,
When back ache premonition,
      Steeps the pains of night away,
Please, remember to come find me,
      We will be stunning,
      We will be young again,
On closed bleached linen sheets,
      You got on sale at Sears,
We will lay together and be whole,
An since your back is curving,
      We will be wild,
      We will be free,
If the brace you buy fails,
      Please, do not let it cripple,
          Your ability to remember me

Chris Minato
San Jose, CA

49

Peace

In life's darkest hour
When life seems bitter,
Seems sour,
Smell a pretty flower.

Through all your fears
And all your tears
Strangely, love appears.

Through all your pains
And endless rains,
Hope sustains.

Sit on a rock, feel free.
Look out to sea.
Wonder, wander, just be

Alfred Burgreen
Brooklyn, NY

These Tears Are Not Just Made Of Water and Salt

These tears are not simply made
Of water and salt
And its endless spills are not
Rivers nor oceans—
Although they are indeed drowning

These tears although simple in molecular form
Have far great depths,
Than one might perceive

These tears although clear and transparent
Have far greater shades
Than one might perceive

Red, blue, green, and black
Are the real culprits, the true colors
Behind these glorious tears

These tears, so flowing
And seemingly full of life
Are the result of all the negativity
Unleashed from that dark bitter soul
Which has entrapped me into that continuous darkness
Which I long to escape

Maria-Ximena Alsina
Los Angeles, CA

For the Love Of "Old Stub"

Head hanging down, eyes big and brown,
stub of a tail barely seen,
Spirit crushed, afraid to be touched,
his pleading eyes spoke to me,
As I scooped him up and hugged that pup,
his furry body wriggled with glee.
Instantly, his attitude warmed my heart,
and he escaped that cold shelter with me.
For fifteen years my loyal friend,
was my very best company,
But today, old and frail, that little stub of a tail,
finally stopped wagging for me.
God holds him gently for me now,
till one day when we'll meet again,
Then I'll scoop him up and I'll hug my pup,
and we'll share eternity as best friends.

Helena B. Schildknecht
Crestwood, KY

The Mystery of Love

The mystery of love, may never be known,
Since the beginning of time, it has grown and grown.
You can't rid your mind, of the loves of your past,
   It plays no favorites, and the arenas are vast.

The mystery of love, leans heavy on your pride,
   Very hard to control, once buried inside.
It's like invisible magic, unseen and mysterious,
When it happens to lovers, it makes them delirious.

The mystery of love is a beautiful event,
The happening is spontaneous, the time is well spent.
Sometime in the future, you will soon discover,
   That fate has dealt you, a mysterious lover.

The mystery of love, will forever remain,
An adventure for people, who can endure the pain,
   Of falling in love, and thinking it is forever,
While the mystery of love, keeps going on forever.

Willie E. Jackson
Milwaukee, WI

53

Alone

As the world spins under my feet
and the single tear leaves my cheek
I reminisce of that special day
that my wish shall come true from
that alone pray
I wished upon that star so bright
that my life would change that
lonely night
as my arms spread wide upon the air
I closed my eyes and wished someone
would care
when I realized my life has stopped
that single planet up under my feet
dropped
I cried, I hurt for that day to come
for someone to tell me I am not alone
No one could help me only I and I alone
My eyes have opened so I could see
see no world beneath me I was free
not free from pain nor sorrow
but free and alone like and unborn child...

Amber N. Gillespie
Allentown, PA

Salute to a Matjes Herring

Fish from the sea
    are not new to me,
But the Matjes herring so sublime,
    has a taste unique,
    truly divine.
As the salt leaves my lips
    and travels to my hips,
I wonder and say,
"Eating this fish
    truly makes my day!"

Charlotte Bornstein
Levittown, NY

Until the End

I keep trying each day to do all I can to be a better man,
with you by my side to add strength I'll make a bold stand;
not trying to make you feel bad, nor to put you on the spot;
You are my support system whether you know it or not;
You've become a part of my "new life," you I will always need,
You gave me something that all men need to be productive and to
succeed;
You've been more than my lover, you are my very best friend,
I'll always be here for you my love, until the very end...

K. Vincent Bailey
Baltimore, MD

55

A Broken Soul

My heart aches from the things my eyes have seen.
My soul is torn from the things my hands have done.
My mind is numb from the things my body has experienced.

Hope is a thing I cannot have.
Faith is just a shattered reality of the person I once was.
Love has become incomprehensible.

Will I ever be anything more?
Can I ever be forgiven?
How can I expose my tormenting demon?

You, oh Lord, have made me for your pleasure.
Why do you allow my torment?
Has the joy of my birth equaled the horrors I am?
I long to sing your praise, and yet, I am cursing my existence.

But, only you know the full story of a person.
Only you can balance justice and mercy.
Forgive my actions.
Forgive my heart.
Teach me once again to love, to love You.

Todd R. Olsen
Levittown, PA

Proserpine

In Maine, lemonade meant July's warm breath,
Our stands like those out of old picture books.
But Chicago had no sweet citrus summers,
Only a widower among harrowing crowds,
Dry heat and the worse half of childhood.
My father replaced the smell of salt with that of smoke.

When my mother cut a lemon, its fresh sting kissed her lips,
Traced the shape of her mouth like an omen. She bit anyway.
I realize our burning eyes were nothing to her,
Not when the cool ocean floor seemed so welcoming.
She ate the seeds and in Hades shall remain,
An Iron Queen waiting fruitlessly to forget and be forgotten.

William Oliver
Duxbury, MA

Unveiled

I remember the night we met; how could I forget?
Your eyes met mine, your arms reached out, your heart, you opened wide.
Your face, your smile, your inner-core; oh, but we'd met before.

From that night on, you ignited a flame deep inside me.
We connected, joined, we became one. Our love, so pure.
Embarking on life's path, hands embraced, hearts secure.
Whatever the journey, our love did endure.
We shared our goals, painted our dreams, hopes we did confide.
We laughed, frolicked, played; magic castles in the sky we made.

Your life has enriched me, your legacy uplifts me.
Those gifts, so cherished and so dear.
Forever, you're with me, no matter how far or how near.
Your life, so generous, infinite, you did impart,
To me, to treasure, together or apart.

Our dreams for our future become memories of our past;
You face, warmth, smile…visions that will always last.
I resolve: as day fades to night and the seasons evolve,
My beloved husband and mate; I turn to nature and fate;
my beloved, my friend, I know, I'm sure, we'll be together again.

Joyce D. Block
Lafayette Hill, PA

On Faith

I've not found faith, although I've tried
I've researched and discovered all have something to hide.
From God to nothing did I see
I thought nirvana won
But that too died, because I lied.
Then suddenly my I saw my inner eye
My inner soul saw the light
Revealed the truth to me
There is no beginning and no end in sight.

Lucille Gorton
Wilton, CT

Nature

When the sun rises strong and bright,
It gives us all a heavenly sight,
Birds, plants, creatures, seas,
To any of you who really see,

So to those who pollute the air,
And whose hearts and eyes are filled
With nothing but despair,
They will never see what is right—
That nature is on the early flight

Rasheedah Shardow
Croton on Hudson, NY

59

Omaha Beach

I stand in awe and wonder as I look out from the shore,
And see the waves roll silently—
Remembering.

The darkest of nights, the slimmest of chances,
The cry of death, but not of defeat—
Remembering.

The sounds of the bullets, machine guns and bombs,
Fellow soldiers dying on the sand—
Remembering.

The endless hours fighting, the toll so high,
It causes me to pause—
Remembering.

The purpose of the battle, to free a land oppressed,
I cannot forget it—
Remembering.

The joy of victory, pulled from tragedy beyond words,
What a blessed relief—
Remembering

Sixty years plus, history moves on.
This shall not be forgotten—
As long as I remember.

Miriam Sturgeon
Harleysville, PA

The Brown Recliner

You sat in a worn brown recliner chair,
the one with the hand control that adjusted positions.
As a little girl, I would crawl up in your lap,
hold up the sports page of the day
and read you stories of what was happening
in the Big Ten.

When I was ready to climb down
you'd lower the chair for me.
I would scurry down the hall
while you watched, silently begging
to have the functioning legs that I did.

I could hear the hum of the motorized chair lying
back into position. And ESPN Sports Center
began commentary from the television.

Days were spent like this. You wanted to teach me
how to play ball like on T.V., but you were bound
by the brown Lazy-Boy. The springs of the seat grew weak
from day-long sitting, and the motor started to lose
power. The droning of sports shows turned
into a soundtrack of home.

That July the television was turned off. The chair was sold.
The sports paper went unread. And my young legs aged
as I walked from the church to the cemetery.

Darci Kirby
Lafayette, IN

Party of One

I sit next to you and sometimes
When I look up it is two hours later.
I feel you next to me more than I see you next to me.
In these moments all that we have shared in our lifetimes
Is drawn to a perfect pitch, an instant almost still
While the rest of time moves on.
You can almost touch it.
I think it must feel comfortable,
If there were a way to apply thought to it.
It is almost like some new being, created in a room,
By the two people sitting next to each other.
The two people sitting in the room are you and me,
Reading, listening to music, the new being is a third person.
And it's you and me, at peace, in peace.
There is really nothing for me to do,
To want to be, nowhere else I'd rather be
Than next to you. Being…with you.

Phil Canalin
Alameda, CA

Vets Hospital

The sign says "Cancer Ward" in big black letters.
No mistaking your diagnosis here.
Maybe less dreadful if it said "Oncology."
But there it is…in practical language.

Out front they have all these makeshift barriers.
It is for construction of a new lovely entry?
Probably not…more likely it is to keep car bombs out.
The building looks like the courthouse in Oklahoma City.

I'll just drop my old soldier off here in the road.
He knows the way to the "Cancer Ward".
And he can still walk, his surgery isn't till Friday.
He'll be glad to see his roommates…chatty old soldiers.

Old soldiers have their own world.
You and I can't go there. It is for the chosen few.
Their surgeons teach at the University
Their caregivers are skillful and international.

So now I can ponder those barricades again.
I can pray for a good outcome.
And I can turn around and go home.
And I hope all these tears don't blind me.

Nona Eschbach
Medina, WA

63

Nothing Compares To You

I love to dance
I love to sing
I love to smell the many flowers
      in the Spring
But with everything I like to do...
      Nothing compares to you
I love the smell of coffee brewing
      When I wake early in the morning
I love the sound of summer rain
      As it beats upon my window pane
But with everything I like to do...
      Nothing compares to you
I love to look up in the sky
      and watch the wild geese fly by
I love to wish upon a star
      and be thankful for the life I've had so far
But with everything I like to do...
      Nothing compares to you
I love to watch the ocean's waves
      and feel the warmth of summer days
To watch lovers in the park
      Sneaking kisses after dark
But with everything I love to do...
      Nothing compares to you
Because there is nothing in this world
      That I would rather do...
        If I couldn't do it all loving you

Alberta Baldassano
Schwenksville, PA

My Hero

As I ponder the love that I saw in his eyes,
A godly love, given without compromise…
I recall many times that he stood by my side,
and prodded me with great vigor and pride.
His voice ever confident, firm and yet fair,
always speaking with patience, tenderness and care.
The power and might of his hands was sure,
I knew there was nothing we couldn't endure.
It's true a few others provided insight,
yet, he laid the foundation that kept me upright.
He's the grandest of men who has lived on this earth,
although he's not royal by stature or birth.
He's a man of great dignity, honor and strength.
His merits are noble, and of admirable length.
he's far greater than all other men that I know,
he's my dad; he's my mentor, my friend and hero.

Marissa Minnis
Roseville, CA

When I Am Ready To Die

When I'm ready to die, let me go.
Let me go peacefully,
Let me go with dignity,
Let me do it my way.
When I'm free, I'll be alive;
I'll be part of the whole universe.
You will see me in the moving clouds,
And see my colors in the rainbow.
You will see me rise and set with the sun,
And, catch my face in the moon, my twinkle in the stars.
You will hear me walk through the autumn woods,
And hear me whisper in the falling rain.
You can listen to my voice in the song of the bird,
And see me unfold in the petal of a flower.
You can witness my spirit in acts of love,
And hear my song in every act of praise.
You can give me the gift of life
Only when you let me go.
And, it is my greatest wish,
When I'm ready to die.

Mae Miner
Port Orange, FL

I grew up in York County and graduated from Northeastern High School, York Hospital School of Nursing and Millersville University. I've been married for 45 years, have a son and two stepdaughters. I spent the last seven years of my nursing career in hospice care. The poem was penned for a gentleman who was having a very difficult time coming to the decision about removing a feeding tube that was keeping his wife alive but causing multiple problems. This poem was instrumental in his decision to remove the feeding tube and allow her to die peacefully. I'm also the author of Pastor Beloved: Finding the Spiritual in Religion.

Winter Wonderland

The wind whips the winter snow
　　into a creamy froth

All though it feels like February
　　It's only January fourth

The snowman smiles from the yard
　　Sympathy he is lacking

Squirrels are having a hard time
　　Finding nuts for snacking

Sleeping croakers lie patiently
　　Waiting to come out

Most animals are hibernating
　　No one is about

Three more months, Spring begins
　　Until then, I'm staying in.

Eileen Fontaine
Westport, MA

G'morning

I see him walking toward me
not a swagger
or a stagger
but something in between
like a man who has had to walk farther than he should
and work harder than he could.

He waves his hand in greeting
then smiles
and begins to shout
"G'morning, G'morning, G'morning!
How are you? My name Buckwin, What's your name?
How you spell?" It's almost always the same!

The day is a much better day because of this
little man
from Viet-nam
with joy enough to spare and share
with those along the way
A special treat that more than brightens up my day!

Marjorie Priest
Seattle, WA

Garden of Wonder

Everywhere you look and see a different color in a tree,
As you look about you see, this is a true menagerie,
There are so many places here, that make you shed a happy tear,
But there is happiness around, with joyful creatures on the ground,
Celestial beings pouring water, to quench the thirst of all,
And as rushing waters sound, these creatures hear its call,
The archway covered in the green, with angels watching waters stream,
With trees of beans and giant leaves that lie upon its breast,
You will find a ladybug calmly take its rest,
So as the fruit trees blossom, as their time begins,
You find a pair of butterflies, fluttering within,
I can see such wonders with the naked eye,
How is it that a paradise has fallen from the sky,
All the leaves reach out with care, as birds are singing all their prayers,
And as I sit in awe of this, I feel I'm in a dream,
As the night floats down upon us, with sparklers of green,
Then look up to the sky above, with diamonds sparkling with his love,
And as the evening becomes dawn, you see a garden full of doves,
I wonder how a single place could give such joy to me,
And as I sit and wonder why and know that it was meant to be.

Kathleen Griffin
Braintree, MA

69

What's In a Word? An Amateur's Plea To Shakespeare

Before thy feet I prostrate lay
A novice of thy poetry art
The words that sing along the way
The elusive word within my heart.

The words that form within my mind
And set the tone for poetry's play
The eluding word, one hard to find
In my limited voice may not lay.

Oh, you, Shakespeare, master of the word
Come now upon my writing lay
The utterance, the right active verb
The sprightliness, the best of the byway.

Florence L. Soldahl
Castro Valley, CA

Daddy

Daddy, bend down a little closer
        So I can grab a hold
For though I stand on tippy-toes
        I hardly see the sun of gold

My heart is overflowing
        I want to appreciate
Things that slip by unseen
        Before it is too late

I want to see the color
        That paints an evening sky
And see the many little stars
        That twinkle in your eye

May I sit upon your shoulders
        I do not weigh too much
I've only fleeting glimpses
        Of wonders to feel and touch

For I am only five years old
        So daddy take my hand
And lift me to you shoulders
        You will be a bigger man

Patsy Sizemore
Baxter Springs, KS

Untitled

I miss you when tomatoes ripe
I remember your joy in every bite
Those luscious garden delights
Not known to market plights.
Uncle Ed called them fruit
He came from the west
Where sugaring tomatoes
He said was best.
You carried salt shaker
In your hip pocket
A feast in your garden
You planned to dock it.
I remember when young
In the neighbors backyard
Those bright luscious goodies
Shone out in the sod. What joy, what delight
When he gave his OK
To share God's gift
That to him was given
With sun and rain
Sent down from Heaven.
I miss you when tomatoes ripe
I remember your joy in every bite.

Lois Sullivan
Jacksonville, FL

Twelve Months

In January, we can build a snowman
In February, we send a valentine
In March, the wind may blow our kite away
In April, the rain may hide the sunshine
In May, we honor our Mothers
In June, we honor our Fathers too
In July, Oh how I love a parade
In August, new flowers bloom for you
In September, the grain starts to ripen
In October, the pumpkins cover the earth
In November, our thoughts turn to Thanksgiving
In December, we celebrate Jesus' birth
After that a New Year begins
And we start all over again

Zencie Rulo
Poplar Bluff, MO

Untitled

This gift to you, I give as a friend,
To enjoy the contents you find within.
God bless and keep you, and happy I'll be,
When you return the empty jar to me.

June Andrews
Ladoga, IN

Keep Hope Alive

Whenever life seems to let you down don't
go around town with a frown. Remember you have
to have hope through your period of trial and to cope.
But through your storm keep hope alive as much as
you may strive the only way to survive is to keep
hope alive. So brothers and sisters when through
life you strive just remember keep hope alive you
surely will survive!

Earl Bynum
Raleigh, NC

My Castle in the air

On empty peaks against the sky
My castle rules the air…
I view its realm with pleasant sigh
Because I know it's there.

It's there! It's there! It's bound to be!
I often hear its call…
It's there and only I can see
Its great majestic sprawl.

It stores my dreams, my wishes too
In hidden treasure rooms…
Where pleasant dreams I then accrue
Again my castle looms.

My airborne castle may deceive,
May alter all my schemes…
Behind some cloud it may take leave
And cancel all my dreams.

But if my dreams become unglued
And vanish into the air,
My castle dream can be renewed
Because—I know it's there!

William T. Smith
Bloomfield, NJ

Going Home

Going home, I'm going home,
Going home today.
Mom and dad will be there
I'm going home to stay.
He was thinking of his childhood
And his kind of life.
Made to mind, went to school
Caused no one any strife.
Thought about the life he has lived
From young man through the years.
Traveled all around as a bum
No doubt caused his mom tears.
Now he's getting old and gray
So he's going home.
It won't be long and he's see
His folks and friends no more.
As he came to a bend
He did not see the car.
It hit him and dragged him
Even though it was not far
Now he's going home, going home
To the one up above.
He does not know he'll see
His mom waiting there with love.

Heleva Bartelote
Lyons Falls, NY

Like a Sister

She is like a sister
She's always there for me
She never leaves me in a fight
Because she knows my needs
She is like a sister because she understands
She always keeps me company even when—
    she has her own plans
She is like a sister because she wipes my tears
And even when I don't ask for it—
    her comfort never wears
She is like a sister because she never fails me
She's always by my side
But sometimes she lets me be
But never does she leave me
For someone else to see
I'm never gonna leave her—
    and she is not gonna leave me.

Like sisters

Olivia Olsen
Rockland, MA

Transformation

Oh lovely leaf
If you could live
To see the
Weary winter months.

Margy Davis
Buckeye, AZ

The Robin

A robin was sitting on a child's swing
It couldn't fly because of a broken wing.
When a little girl came out to play,
the robin could not fly away.
She said, "Oh you poor little thing,
I'll get my mommy to fix your wing,"
With tenderness of loving hands,
She fixed the wing with a little band.
They put it in a box to rest.
So when it's strong it can build a nest.
Every morning, loud and clear
The robin sang for the ones who loved it so dear.

Margaret E. Bonsall
Garnet Valley, PA

The Holiday Season

The warm house protecting me,
With every snow storm that we see,
As the sky spits out snowflakes the size of golf balls,
Carolers happily sing Deck the Halls,
The tree standing there bright with lights,
As the wind blows on cold wither nights,
Mistletoes hung up high,
With many hugs and kisses good-bye,
The smell of Christmas cookies being made,
While decorations are being displayed,
Sneaking out of bed at night,
To see if Santa and his reindeers are anywhere in sight,
Creeping down the stairs on Christmas morning,
While the parents are left in bed snoring
This lovely holiday season is here,
So let's make the best of it and cheer

Nicole Kowalski
Wind Lake, WI

Love's Talk

It has an eloquent tongue
Can speak volumes about
Who it is shared with
But never speaks at all.

It can be sweet, soft, cool,
Demanding, compassionate
Or signal of one's demise.

I can't remember my first,
Hope I haven't had my last.

Exchanged at arrival,
Departure and farewell,
It's your heart's true voice.

John Bassi
Santa Maria, CA

Christmas '08

OMG! What has become of us
It's enough to make us cuss
Two endless wars on our hands
Fought in far-off little-known lands

Our portfolios have all gone South
Making everyone down in the mouth
Unemployment at an all-time high
Many people just want to cry

But the biggest injustice of all
The very epitome of gaul
The Belgians bought out Anheuser-Busch
I hope they fall on their big fat tush

Let's hope the worst is over
And we'll soon recover
Tis the Season to be Jolly
Even if we have wilted Holly

Enough with the Doom & Gloom
Let's pray for a Mini Boom
The Holidays are here and bring joy
Hope Santa Clause brings me a new toy

We hope you all have a nice Season
And circumstances will give us a reason
To look to next year with lots of hope
Making us better able to cope.

Dick Hanson
N. Ft. Myers, FL

81

Salvation Rap

I was lost in sin, consumed by pain…
then I gave my heart to Jesus and was born again
He took me in his arms, He held me tight…
He whispered in my ear "it'll be alright."
He looked at my heart and could see it was pure…
then He looked at my life and said "you need a cure"
There were things in there, not pleasing to His eye…
the wages of sin is you gonna die
Not dying where you go to your heavenly home…
but to a hot burning place where you die all alone
He grabbed me by the shoulders and shouted "change your way…
or you're gonna be sorry come judgment day"
I fell to my knees and admitted my wrong…
He said "you're forgiven, now sister stay strong"
It is not for us to make our own rules…
We must follow Jesus' way or else we're big fools
No matter what you done, you know He loves you still…
That's the point I'm trying to make, his grace is ever real
I beseech thee saints, pay heed to my rhyme…
the end is close at hand and we're running out of time
I'm not trying to preach, God just put it on my heart…
So like I said before just make a fresh start
just praise The Lord, He's a mighty deity…
With Jesus in your life, you will truly be free

Sher Crawford
Brooklyn, NY

I don't like to identify myself by age, race, or geography. I'm a teen-age girl, and a grandmother. I am Black and I am White. I am a citizen of the world. My inspiration comes from The Lord. My poetry is honest and hard hitting, whether I'm writing about God, family, love, or life. My themes are universal.

Stars

When I look up in the sky
in the early morning dawn,
I behold the sight
of the beautiful morning star.

How it helps me remember
all day and throughout my life,
There is someone much greater
than me, myself and I.
Thanks to the seed
that was planted long ago,
To see the star helps my
faith continue to grow.

Then in the evening dusk
I look up in the sky,
I see the brilliant evening star,
so beautiful and so bright.
It reminds me once again
there is someone much bigger than me,
who helps me live my life
to the fullest potential I can be.

I love to see those stars
that shine so bright above,
They help me feel a lot
but mostly, I feel Love.

Lindsey Cosson
St. George, UT

The Literary Circle

A story is an idea
　　that goes for a walk

A poem is a word
　　that leads to a thought

A thought then leads
　　to imagination

which in turn
　　sparks an exaggeration

Exaggeration is
　　the spice of life
Essential as a
　　fork to a knife

All this culminates
　　in tongue and pen

And so
　　the cycle begins again!

Patricia Petronella
Yonkers, NY

My Daddyo

My daddy is the best.
When he smiles
the clouds depart
when he laughs
the rain is no more.
When he tells a joke
time stops turning
He is cool.
He is kind.
He is the ultimate parent.
I want to be just like him.
My Daddyo
owns a special section
of my heart.
He is more important
than the moon
and the sun.
Daddyo is the best Daddyo
anyone could have.

Mariel Andersen
Barboursville, VA

85

Skulls

Shadows of the mind and heart
seek the empty path,
an unmapped trail.
You go on ahead,
through the ghostly forest blindly.
Eat from the snake
and rest under the tree of the dead.
Let the hanging skulls
and decaying heads drape over you
having their maggot filled eyes watch you
for they know the curse of the fruit
for your head will join theirs in time
your heart and body will decay
and your head will hang from the tree
watching as others make your mistake
and all you can do is watch
helplessly…
forever

Jessica Tumlin
Temple, GA

From Heaven

When you are blessed—
      it's from heaven.
When you are anointed—
      it's from heaven.
Like the rain drops—
      it's from heaven.
That touch of hope—
      it's from heaven.
A light will shine—
      it's from heaven.
From heaven,
From heaven.

Gloria Cooper
Powder Springs, GA

A Memory With You

In a park all alone, the wind is whirling around us.
We close our eyes and lean in.
Our lips touch.
I feel the butterflies in my stomach start to rise,
as your grip around my waist tightens.
What feels like hours only seconds pass.
We start to pull away.
We look into each others eyes and smile.
You pull me close and I lay my head against your chest.
You kiss my head and whisper in my ear, "I love you."
I smile as you say that because I wish we could stay this way forever.

Elena Byrne
Fresh Meadows, NY

Letting Go

The car is packed it's time to leave
How fast time has flown it's hard to believe
And though only a few hours away
I'm going to miss her each and every day
Dad's driving she's talking I don't hear a word that's said
Too many memories running through my head.
I can picture her out in the backyard
Playing on the swings and the monkey bars.
An amazing woman she's grown to be
A heart that's filled will hopes and dreams.
It takes all my strength to hold back the tears
For they have been eighteen wonderful years
All too soon we arrive
As we look for her dorm I just sigh
We unpack get her settled a hug and a kiss
Already my daughter I'm starting to miss.
I giver a fake smile she closes the door
By the time I get home I miss her even more.
I walk past her room I can't hold back the tears
For they have been eighteen wonderful years.
It's been a pleasure watching her grow
I'm so proud of her now it's time to let go.

Chris Ziobert
Youngstown, OH

You Make Us Very Proud

Our country needs us, to join as one,
to do our patriotic duties, as others have done.
The bible teaches us, it works every time,
That God is in control, regardless of the crime.
Our soldiers are fighting, with intension to stay,
giving it their best, in each and every way.
American people, we can show the care,
asking God to bless our soldiers, in continuous prayer.
Families set apart, need that extra love too,
let's support our country, the red, white, and blue.
Freedom is the reason, our soldiers had to go,
Helping another country for democracy to grow.
Standing together united we are,
bonded spiritually by God, no matter how far.
The flag flows silent, but sings quite loud,
attention all soldiers you make us very proud.

Susan E. Doss
Saint Peters, MO

Emotion Poem

Pain. Pain. You make me insane.
I can't refrain, can't contain.
Spill forth the absurd, the words of the disturbed,
Not much curbed.
What a loose tongue, still young,
I'm lost among the sound of the drums.
Pounding in my head, never proof-read, but instead, defeated.
Shot down in confusion, a heart and mouth infusion
Led in delusion, my institution.
Why go on? Carry on? Continue on? Just hurry on.
Off on your own, in your silent home
A noiseless drone on microphone.
What can one say when they're in such a way,
That the next day arouses dismay?
To a heart that's falling apart? Distorted art, altered chart.
Easily lost, needlessly crossed,
Paying the cost all shiny and glossed.
Dim is the fire. I see as you tire.
Go ahead and retire, while I expire.
Mulch in the leaves hear the wind breathe.
On nod the trees as they strain to appease.

Tamara Shearer
Beaumont, CA

Clarity

Among the aspens
which speckle a
mountain's valley with
whisperings of life's
peaceful offering,
lies the secret of a
heart's unseen joy;
for having the whisperings
of life within itself.
Soft transparent waters
of the stream glide
through the valley
smiling wisely sparkling
with pride at all
that is within its
realm of reflection.

Maria Marchini
Rome, PA

Gone With God's Love

Life is a struggle every day
Call on God to help God in your heart and soul
Watch your life unfold
The love of God is worth more than gold
So don't stay mad and grumpy until your old
Time and God have no one to answer to
When it's your time to go there is no compromising
Your journey is now complete
And your true father you must meet
Enjoy every moment until your last
Because the life you've lived is now your last
For those whom you care for and love say what you have to say
because you don't know if you'll be blessed with another day
So be thankful for today
And remember to pray
Until that last day

Sherrifa Bennett
Queens Village, NY

Dear Mr. President

It seems we're lost in time, my friend,
And don't you think we're not!
Or have we simply stalled our engines
In the parking lot?

We drove for hours through the storm.
We used the gas we had
And simply ended up in no-man's land: Baghdad
It seems we're lost in time.

The Taliban, the also-rans, and all
Their stereotypes grow dull with age.
Let's find our page!
And let them fade in style!

The North Koreans can rattle themselves
And rattle the rest of the world,
But they're just like a child with a toy.
That's all, but their flag's unfurled.

Perseverance saves their freedom
So don't lose your patience with them.
For Peace is our treasured motto there.
And thank you for listening.

Johanna A. Murphy-Pierce
Oceanside, CA

Guitar Heroine

The sun in that Californian rain.
Or an old, open, rolling plain.
The guitar speaks its melody
And resonates somewhere inside of me.
If I really knew how to play,
Play I would all summer's day.
In my brain, I've got my tune,
But I just can't get my fingers to move.
If this were something logical, I might just study.
But it's not, for music needs to be free.
How do I do this? Do I pick it up and start to learn?
Or do I join a group and wait my turn?
I want to play, but all I do is sing…
Sing songs about how I wish I could do this thing

Rachael Jones
Aliso Viejo, CA

Feed the Hungry

they stand with bellies fat
but empty
the little brown children of
struggling Darfur.

you hear the constant wail,
not crying,
for crying requires energy
they have lost.

in America, they sleep under
highway bridges
and by day wander the
dirty streets.

our hearts and minds cry
for you
you reply with pleading eyes,
"feed me."

WAILING.   PLEADING.

silence

Ruth J. Hilleke
Highland Heights, KY

The Boy in a Fur Suit

I adopted my son we bonded quickly
The boy's magic touched my heart a love spell that let me know
we would always be together and never part
The boy has a kind, gentle, strong, stubborn and bold soul
The boy is nurtured with children
Nieces, nephews, and granddaughters galore
The boy's sister calls him brother, whom the whole family adores
The boy is praised and put on a pedestal
For those who cross his path always take the time to recognize
Pat the lad's head and then succumb to kneel at his feet
The boy opened my mind to explore a world of wonder adventure
The boy is a teacher to me of many sorts
The boy teaches me patience, gentleness, and to be true to my feelings
which had to be
Freed to embrace innocent creatures
The boy shows me the way to love all breeds no matter their decree
The boy gives me a voice, a voice to be heard to speak with
a kind word, animals
Should not be bought, sold, abused, or used they should be
cherished, loved and for mankind to hold
The boy in a fur suit gave me a gift the best I ever could receive
when he blessed me to be his mommy

Lisa L. Lucas
Williamsport, PA

Until recently I lived with my son and beagle, named Boy. Boy gave us twelve years
shared of loyalty and companionship, they will be shared and treasured in my mind and
heart. I was inspired to write this poem through my own experience of raising a beagle.
The beginning of his life he was loved, respected, and he reciprocated the feelings to
others from his big brown eyes, to the smile upon his face, and the warm kisses. I
discovered that I am a true animal lover from being made aware of the animal world.

Untitled

Today it was yellow, before that it was blue,
I'm hoping your colors reflect no one but you.
Somewhere a flower is blooming, its colors are bright,
Its petals are open and provide such a sight.
The leaves are now orange, no longer green,
Mixed with some yellow gives off a warm scene.
When it rains the sky turns a dreadful gray,
After the sun peeks through, it brings color to the day.
Whether it's the color of the valleys, or the color of the sea,
Your smile is as colorful as it can be.

Asiya Mahmood
Brooklyn, NY

Untitled

December twenty-fifth.
Streets deserted,
Buildings dark,
Everyone asleep.
From the thirtieth floor,
With classical music and
An unfiltered cigarette,
I watch the snow
Fall gently on the city.

Alfred Morris
New Canaan, CT

Eternity

Don't cry Mommy, Daddy's in Heaven and he can't come home;
he never meant to die and leave us alone.
We were all young and full of tears,
living our lives without him for the rest of our years.

For now we are no longer children, but young adults.
Time has gone on, but he is still in our thoughts.
The memories we share,
remind us that he cared.

His work was completed,
but we felt we were cheated.
His life is gone,
but we remain strong.

I may not remember everything,
but I know his love still remains.
I look to the sky,
and know he is by.

Life's journey has its twists and turns.
The years continue to flee and churn.
I know someday my life will pass;
I will join my Dad at last.
Into his arms I'll never leave;
what a reunion eternity will be.

Cindy K. Brown
Ansonia, OH

I grew up in a small rural village in Ohio. Kris A. Brown became the village Chief of police at the age of 21. We were married three years later. We had three children, Kristopher, Heather, and Jessica. In 1990, Kris died at the age of 34 while working for the village. Our children were eight, six, and two. I prayed for the words to write this poem for them, I've seen and felt their pain. The day Kris died, Jessica told me "Don't cry Mommy, Daddy's in Heaven and can't come home."

Wishes

Wish you and all that joy may outweigh grief
>May light eclipse the dark
>Be strong and brave
>Let courage leave its mark.

Wish you and all that health feverishly infect sickness
>May beauty radiate with light upon the ugliness of night
>May art oppress oppression and iron shackles bind regret
>May freedom reign above tyranny and loudly ring its Bell

Wish you and all that fortunes rain and drench the deserts of despair
>That ecstasy and faith electrify the one too numb to care
>May sensuality exalt and vindicate the truth
>Let creativity burst the ramparts of stagnation

Wish you and all that gladness plows the fields of melancholy way
>And that humility despoils vain, decadent conceit
>That Brotherhood and Sisterhood break thru the walls of—
>Separation
>And Justice inter injustice in a deep dungeon of concrete

Wish you and all that hope fulfills the heart
>Bridge all and everything apart
>And may none ever come too late
>May love forever outweigh hate…

Arnold Zilban
Far Rockaway, NY

"...Each divine spark yearns to reconcile itself with Eminence and Emanation of its original, sacred fire...." Born and partially raised in the Soviet Union and as a consequence of then atheist regime, I grew up in the secretive, outlawed and fragmented Judaic culture. During adolescence I was drawn to kabalistic poetry that's richly interspersed in liturgical Judaism. The inspiration for "Wishes" … it is an ode to humanity's yearnings. I wrote "Wishes" as a cathartic exercise to purge the bitter disappointment of an unrequited romantic interest. I sent it to her anyway!

Snowflakes

You know they say there never are,
two snowflakes just the same.
That's how I feel when I look at you,
with such love I can't explain.
I will not try to fool myself
into believing there are two.
There's only one that can have my love,
and there will never be
another one quite like you—
Who can share their love with me.
And if somebody you should melt away,
the only thing I see
is a heartbroken, lonely crying girl,
for her love that's meant to be.

Brandi Emery
Kersey, CO

Bless Each Day

Do you bless each day, each week, each year, do you have a path That is crystal clear. In times of stress do you still feel blessed, in times Of hurt and pain, do you feel any gain. In times of joy and happiness do You understand the gifts we each have been given, do you care and do You share.

Do you pray to one God or maybe two, are you a Christian or maybe A Jew. Does it really matter how we share and care, do you know in Your heart, for Friends and family, you'll always be there.

It's a real gift to know the person on your left and the person on Your right, The one down the street and the person you are about to Meet. Sharing your thoughts, others sharing theirs, the good, the bad, The joy, the pain, builds a friendship, a family, a community, and we All gain. Open your mind, open your heart, bless each day and you will Find, yes you just might find, what you are looking for.

Thomas Dutcher
Allentown, PA

Broken Heart

Once there was a light in my heart
It no longer shines
The girl I truly love is no longer mine,
So I sit by bed
Reading to pray
Hoping Jenny will return one day.
For in my heart I'll never forget,
God bless the day we met.

Kenneth Vickers
Brockton, MA

Beginning the End

Nearby the end of life's waters
Beginning the struggle to pass over
The deep dark waters
No complaints of the forwarding journey
Understanding and love wait on the
Dry land of hope.
Your soul begins its sacred journey
To meet the end of being and
Pass into eternity.
No pain. No end.
Beginning a new life with the
Love of a friend.

Lenora L. Chester
Moscow, PA

Light

Dawn with its sprinkles of light
Slipping between the fingers of her outstretched hands
Every particle that ever made its way down
Down, down, to the vast and looming fields of this earth.
The shine that erupts in a glow too blinding for her squinting eyes;
The light that is deemed harsh against the black background of
    humanity.

The light that falls in through the cracks of the shell that surrounds
    the dark world
The small rays that fall on the looming shadows of man,
The figures that would be non-existent were it not for that light and
    those shadows
And a perfect medley of each.

The dark and dirty cloth that surrounds the earth
Casting an ominous darkness over its inhabitants.
The stars illuminated from the outside by an unknowable source,
Their twinkles pouring in from between the close stitches.

The misfortunes that humanity endures
Caused by woman's follies or man's greed;
The constant blame and bickering that lead to nothing
With the absence of light do all things end.

Fatima Hosain
Hopewell Junction, NY

Hopes for Summer

Snowflakes drift
From the chimneys, smoke rises
Winter never brings any surprises
It's always the same
Bleak, white, and cold
Not like summer
Hot, loud, and bold
Summer brings joy
Like camp and swimming
Winter brings boredom
Like shoveling and shivering
How I long to be outside
Wild and free
I don't like what winter makes of me
In the winter I am nothing but a cold piece of dust
But in summer I'm a giant, loud and robust
Outside I see only the fog
Not a single flower, leaf, or frog
Nothing bubbling with excitement or joy
Only the vanished footsteps of a playing little boy
Please leave winter
You bring nothing but cold
Please come summer
With stories untold.

Alexandra Wieser
Cortlandt Manor, NY

January Born

A man named Martin, January born
Would soon become a symbol for his race,
Uniting the country; their morals torn.

This division stemming from people's scorn;
Discrimination, oh what a disgrace.
Blacks started to fight back, their presence worn.

Dr. King would soon become quite a thorn
In the sides of those anti-color of face;
A man who colored folk would soon adorn.

A person with a dream, never forlorn,
Making Lincoln Memorial the place
That would make justice granted, freedom sworn.

That man named Martin, January born,
Discrimination he dreamed to erase.
His beliefs never changed or became worn.

Shot on April 4, but his dream not torn.
Now all races, our country does embrace.
A man whom we commemorate and mourn,
Never forgotten. January born.

Jacqueline Leake
Woodbine, MD

Metamorphous

To me you are a kaleidoscope
A multi-faceted personality
With constantly changing colors
Prisms of behavior patterns
That emerge as sudden, bright,
And glorious hues only to explode
Into infinite variables
Converging into a rich rainbow
Of dashing primary prints
Yet soft, sweet, gentle pastels
Emboldened with grays and blacks
Sudden bursts of glowing orange
And fiery passionate reds
How I would like to harness
Some of these charismatic views
But each colored glass, alas
Is caught up in a slithery blend
Of ever-revolving constants
With every twist of my wrist
I recognize I cannot control
But only gaze in wonder and in awe.

Millicent J. Summers
Silver Spring, MD

The Prairie Life

My eyes have seen the barren land
Where not even with a thousand hands
Could the ground be turned into a garden.
My hands have touched the tainted earth
Where every day a woman gives birth
To the only crop that grows here.

The burning sun has scorched the ground
And the rampant wind is the only sound
That one can hear at night when all is still.
What trees that live are slowly dying
And as I hear the newborn crying
I think perhaps we'll get some rain tomorrow.

But life goes on, in this our prairie life
And all I have left is a loving wife
Who hasn't complained for nigh on thirty years.
This land I own can't be the land of plenty
For there isn't really very many
Things that we can hope to grow.

Stanley McAdams
E. Stroudsburg, PA

Untitled

Lord I don't know,
What to do or say,
Want to be a free man,
And go about my way.

Lord I want,
To do the best I can,
And try to offer,
A helping hand.

Lord I want,
To forget about my past.
By starting from the beginning,
And then to the last.

Lord I want,
My troubles to go away,
And be a better person,
To this very day.

Lord I want to get along,
With others like I should,
And willing to do other things,
If I knew I could.

Lord I want to know,
The things that are true,
And also realizing,
That my love is for you.

James Hudson
Fayetteville, GA

Just Too Busy

Alas my youth has long passed by
So I sit and rock and often sigh
For the bygone "should haves"
And countless "could haves"
That I was too busy—or too blind—to try
Opportunity has often knocked in vain
For I was too busy to think how I'd gain
Good chances flew by to return no more
And I was too busy to open the door
You may think I should weep
But that is not so
For good thoughts I still keep
Help to ease all that woe.

Barbara Cole
Santa Ana, CA

To My Kids

The day will come when
I must leave this world
    To move into the next world,
I will have to leave you
    I will hold onto this world
For as long as I can
    I will always be in your heart
Remember that
    I will always be at your side
And here is how you will know
    When the wind whips around you,
That will be me wrapping my arms around you
    When the sun shines on your face
And gives you a warm feeling
    That will be my hands holding your face up
So all can see your beauty
    When you hear or see things move
And cannot explain it.
    That will be me trying to bring a smile to
Your face with my strange humor
    Remember I will always be with you.

Venett Martin
Phoenix, NY

The Deadly Sting

When love was young and here and now
And night and day my heart just sang
I never contemplated how
The pleasure might become this pang.

I carried on in lovers' bliss
I treasured every tender word
Not knowing something was amiss
And not expecting what occurred.

And now that love is lost and gone
And days are difficult and dim
I'm overwhelmed by what went on
By passion spent, by losing him.

How strange that love so wondrously
Can captivate, be promising
Then, later, unexpectedly
Deliver me this deadly sting.

Gloria J. Gorman
Vista, CA

His Love Filled Face

Behind the smile the face the clothes
Is a girl whose life has completely froze.
A mask is what she hides behind
Thee answers to life she can't find.
Everything passes a hazy cloud blur
She constantly wanders why it's happening to her.
Self-conscious about everything from head to toe
Trusting no one she won't let her feelings show.
Everyone seems so happy and real
She wonders why her own sorrows won't heal.
Her life seems unwritten unscripted unplanned
She walks around aimlessly ignoring his hand.
But still he waits patiently day after day
But feels his heart ache when she walks the other way.
He watches her search from place to place
Ignoring his heart and love-filled face.
For he would die, yes, he loves her that much
He waits for the day she'll accept his touch.
Until then he will wait, yes he will wait
He'll watch from a distance help her up when she falls
Until she discovers finally for herself—
The greatest love of all.

Hannah B. Coffman
Yacolt, WA

112

Shattered

Why must my life feel shattered most of the time
I'll try to put my feelings in this rhyme
I danced today this makes me smile
Only for a moment only for a while
I feel lost in guilt for love, family and friends
Wisemen say you can't hold it in you must make amends
I resort to a child-like state
Innocence I pray will be my fate
So I say to parents that have scars so deep
Children do inherit and so they will weep

Annette Nead
Lakeland, FL

Untitled

We were meant for each other
It was always planned that way
We should love one another
As we have this very day
When away from you dear
I think of all the fun
Of the times when you were near
And of all the things we've done
And as the years roll by
When we are forced to part
I'll know that you are here
And still in my heart

Sandra Sponsel
Shelbyville, IN

113

Strictly Germproof

The antiseptic baby and the prophylactic pup,
Were playing in the garden, when a bunny gambled up.

They looked upon the creature with a loathing undisguised,
It wasn't disinfected and it wasn't sterilized.

They said it was a microbe and a hotbed of disease,
They steamed it in a vapor of a thousand odd degrees.

They froze it in a freezer that was cold as banished hope,
They washed it in permanganate with carbolated soap.

In sulphurated hydrogen they steeped its wiggly ears,
They trimmed its frisky whiskers with a pair of hard-boiled shears.

They donned their rubber mittens and took it by the paw,
And elected it a member of the fumigated all.

Now, there's not a micrococcus in the garden where they play.
They bathe in pure iodoform, a dozen times a day.

And each imbibes his rations from a white hygienic cup,
The bunny, the baby, and the prophylactic pup.

Ron Myers
Tucson, AZ

My moment

The colors are illuminating, heightened
appear alive, new . . .

Shades of greens, yellows, reds, oranges
and true blues . . .

White puffy clouds, streaks of pink
against steel gray skies . . .

So many wonders of this world
once I opened my eyes . . .

The moment has arrived after long
days of not knowing . . .

My present is now filled with wonderment
always glowing . . .

If I could pass it on to you, this
new moment of mine . . .

Hold out your hand, it's my pleasure
to introduce you to All that is divine.

Linda Shores
Lovettsville, VA

A Christmas Prayer

Mary my soul's bright Morning Star
Shining when other stars grow dim
Now in the quiet of the dawn
Lead me to Him!
You who gave birth to Christ our King
Let me approach Him on this day
Though I am lost I beg your help
Show me the way!
Mary I stand alone and wait
Give me your hand my Mother dear
Whisper to Him as He awakes
Tell him I'm here!
Mary my soul's bright Morning Star
Hear me dear Mother as I pray
Ask Him to bless, forgive and love
All of us on this Christmas Day!
Amen

Ruth Farabaugh
Manlius, NY

Do You Really Believe?

Do you really believe?
Do you know
Are you sure
Was a seed planted
Making reason
Obscure?

Do you really believe?
Do you care
If it's true
The seed on a mission
Rooted deep
As it grew.

Do you really believe?
Depend upon faith
Rely upon trust
The seed is a plant
Deciding
What's just.

Do you really believe?
No judgment
No thought
The plant now a tree
A lesson
Well taught!

Bernard Stone
Monroe Township, NJ

117

Snowfall

Snow swirling fiercely
Scurries past the window pane
Stubbornly clinging to sills…
Inching upward, in chilly accumulation.

Snow blinding eyes
Freezing faces that peer out
Individual, crusted flakes . . .
Falling in quiet, mad abandon.

Snow so bright
A pure white cover
Pouring down to blanket . . .
Every inch, in its own clean pattern.

Snow as it rages wildly
Shifts and drifts in odd paths
Stinging, stranding helpless life . . .
While icing roofs, with over-hanging scallops.

Snow engulfing pine trees
Layers them in lacey tiers
Wet pigeons perch upon chimney tops . . .
Gathering smoky warmth, against the cold.

Snow . . . Beautiful . . . snow lingers
And somehow protects new life . . .
Lying dormant far below earth's crust . . .
Awaiting Nature's rebirth of spring

Mary Dixon
Zanesville, OH

I am a senior citizen and I have been writing poetry for many years. I find it a release that takes me to a happier place, to enjoy a beautiful "Snowfall."

A Loving Tribute to My Parents

I went to the store to buy a card,
but finding one was very hard.
None of them could quite convey,
the words my heart really wanted to say.
You're special, loving and so very dear
and helped me to overcome my every fear.
Life is hard and sometimes unfair,
But you and Dad have always been there,
To pick me up when I fall,
To love and encourage me most of all.
Mere words could never really express,
The way I feel my life's been blessed.
Not only are you my parents, you're my friends,
And on you both do I depend.
The love you give me cannot be measured,
But in my heart it will forever be treasured.

Peggy Schafer
Elkhorn, WI

Autism Looks Like

What does Autism look like? It looks like me.
Welcome to my Queendom. Come one, come all, come see
My brain is wired differently as my normal body grows
Actions, ideas, don't talk, I obsess, I'm nervous, I can't let go
Sometimes I look real crazy, I feel real crazy too
There's a lot to hear and understand; it's hard to get a clue
I can be overly sensitive, stuff rubs me the wrong way
I understand what you say to me but I don't know what to say.
I day dream a lot, hear music play, create adventure in my mind.
I'm smart and I can learn a lot when people are patient and kind.
My body grows strong and tall like most other girl and boys.
Autism makes me see and hear differently that's my special joy.
School, parents, homework, chores stress me, I wish it all were easy.
God gave me friends, teachers, a school and peeps to keep it "breezy."
Hot cold up down in out unfocused thoughts race I can't sit still.
Just in time "my angels" surround me with a love calm confidence refill.
I like movies, Playstation, Disneyland and the mix that makes you move
I love no homework, being included, smiling faces, Buenos Dias, "Let's
Groove."
Autism, Aspergers, Deaf, Hyper, ADHD, It's hard to win.
Keep helping me please, I appreciate you,
Thank you for letting me be myself again.
What does autism look like? It looks like me.

Kimberley LeMelle
Studio City, CA

120

I Am Me

I fly through this tunnel
looking down upon what I cannot
see, feeling weary I begin to fall;
down into the deepest depths of me.

Upon my descent into the catacomb
of my life, floating in the dark I find
a brilliant crystal mirror, with the
reflections of my life scattered across its face
leaving my purpose so much clearer.

Who am I? Who do I want to be? Were
questions that riddled my mind for decades
When in truth the answer was staring at
me in spades.

For I am me! I only want to be me!
I am happier when I am myself
and saddened when I attempt to be
someone who isn't me!

Jen Nelson
Hubbard, OH

The Life and Death of Danby Rivers

This morning Danby Rivers was quite surprised
when he tried to wake, but instead realized
that during the night he had met his demise.

So, head in hands, Danby sat and wept
and into his heart, disappointment crept
for, as in his life, through death, he'd slept.

True to form and pattern cast,
no one noticed that he had passed
and then awake, Danby was at last.

But time is not always a friend,
for, though it sees you through to end,
it will waste with you in should-have-been.

When Danby finally laid to rest,
between Earth's arms, upon Earth's breast,
he believed his fate was for the best.

Which is why his death came years too soon
blossoming until it bloomed
and burst from his chest, where it took root
and kept itself well disguised
within a masque called Danby's life
that was born too late, once he had died.

For Danby Rivers, though, hearts need not ache
for Danby Rivers choices did make
that atop Danby Rivers forever lay.

Brandelyn M. Hilgefort
Greenville, OH

Musical Tractor

My motor is slow
My paint is rusted and peeled
I don't plant or sow
I only set in a field.
Has everyone forgotten me?
It has been so long
Since someone turned my key
To hear my sweet song

Barbara Nicholas
Tuscon, AZ

How Far

I walked along the edge of the water
a strange cool mist rose. I looked to
see how far it ran, but I did not dare
to follow far.
So I sat beside the edge of the water
the deep blue waves lapped my toes.
I looked deep into the water,
but it was far too deep for me.
I watched the sunset into the water
the bright red, orange and yellow.
I wondered how far it would fall but
I did not dare to follow.

Anne Ouellette
Jay, ME

Snow Is Cold

We're sitting here just the two of us,
    the cat and me.
We can't see out the window because
    of the gust
Staying inside for us is a must
Snow, snow, and more snow is all
    we can see.
A picture is set in our minds
    at least of a ground covered with a
    white blanket.
The neighborhood children with shovels
    and snowballs and their Frosty I bet.
A car has slid off the road and
    is being towed away.
The driver rides in the police car
    in quiet dismay.
My porch steps are covered in snow,
    drifts appearing as in straight rows.
The pond is covered and my shrubs
    are white.
The post on my mailbox doesn't
    look quite right.
So, even though our imagination
    is all we've got, freezing cold
    we're not!

Donna Dumas
Constable, NY

Laying Of Christmas Wreaths

Old vets in pieces of uniforms
Cub scouts in bright red caps;
The show goes on in spite of the rain
The bugler is blowing taps.

We're here today to honor the dead
With flags blowing in the cold.
There's a roar as jets fly overhead,
While tales of valor are told.

Marines have dropped the flag to half mast,
The chaplain is praying for peace.
With tears in our eyes we think of the past,
If only the fighting would cease.

And all our warriors come home to stay
Families would be whole again
The soldiers and sailors would all stand down
There would be an end to the pain.

Kent B. Hake
Jerseyville, IL

Fairies Dance

One day I took a walk.
I looked up at the trees.
I saw some pretty blue jays and some yellow bees.

As I stood there and let out a sigh,
I sat and watched the blue jays fly
And build their nest beautifully.

Then they started to sing and flew on by.

I spied a clump of dotted mushrooms;
Underneath were living fairies.

They were dancing for their dinner,
The children eating berries.

I turned and headed home and left my fairy friends.
But I will come back tomorrow to see my friends again.

Amber Campbell
Rapid City, SD

Our Mother

Our mother passed away
So many years ago
She never got to see
All her children grow

Now we're all adults
With children of our own
If only we could see her
To show her how we've grown

And show her all her grandchildren
That she would love so dear
She could see how much they've grown
Over all the years

Someday we'll meet again
In Heaven up above
Where we can all be together
And catch upon our love

Until that day is here
That we see her once again
We'll all be together
And go on until the end

If all the mothers in the world
Were all as great as ours
This world would be a perfect place
And as beautiful as ours

Stella M. Bruss
Bellefonte, PA

127

Mirror

There is nothing you can say or do to make my heart feel changed.
For now I live in sorrow, and for you there is my blame.
Now anger fills my throat and sickness I do smell.
For my love that once I valued now burns in my own hell.
Nothing but a mirror of thy self, you now shall only see.
For never a colder man as you, shall see the sight of me.

Now you are death becoming, and your skin shall crawl with hate.
And in your heart is darkness, and Hell shows on your face.
You are nothing now, but death's own child, vain and selfish as the sea.
You're shallow as my empty stomach, burning with you now deceased.
Feeling fear of you, my own devil, not deserving a tear.

And so now to me, you are nothing.
I can't see you, angers passed.
Now forgotten are you young devil.
And broken is my reflecting glass.

Stephanie Thacker
Blacklick, OH

God's Messenger

Whatever happened to the human race,
as we walk toward the sunset of our
lives in disgrace. Whatever happened
to the things we did and the things
we failed to do to live in God's ways
and love and help each other, as
sisters and brothers, all over the world.
May God forgive us for the things
we done and the things we failed
to do, the good things we done
are far and very few.
So let's get back to helping others
and don't forget we are all sisters and
brothers
so with God's help, let us show
each other.
Let's help the poor, the hungry,
and the sick.
God bless us all.

Alfred Schmitz
Bedford, OH

The Restless Time

Now is the restless time…
Confusion rules your mind.
For years she's been there…
Always for you, all the time.
Now your wandering eyes see…
Your future and to you,
She's not in the plan…
All the tears have been cried;
She's making plans alone…
Yes, it is the restless time!

Yes, it is the restless time…
You're not sure what you'll do.
Others reach deep into your life…
Shutting out the dreams of your wife.
So throw away all that you have…
You'll realize someday what's gone.
It'll be too late for you then…
So chase your dreams, make your plans,
While you're so far away from her…
Now is the restless time!

Florence M. Perry
Ormond Beach, FL

Ode to Life

Life is an obstacle course
you have so many decisions to make
it just makes it worse
and all it does is make you shake
cause you're all nerves inside
not wanting to make a mistake
but you don't know what to do
and you feel like you're tied
with all the things you take
into your life for you

Carmen Johnson
Zebulon, NC

Reality Dream

Yellow is the sun which shines down on me.
White is the clouds which float up above.
Blue is the sky which just surrounds me.
Why oh why can't you be mine?
I dream about you every night and wake up with you too.
I wonder how long it will take
To make my dreams come true.
So surround me with the sky so blue,
And let shine down the sun of gold,
Pictured on the clouds so bold,
Let me be there with you.

Denise Lang Romero
New Hyde Park, NY

You With Your Child, Me Without

I watched you from my kitchen window
You with your child
Me without

I watched your silhouette of mother and child
You casually lulled across your living room floor
Your child nestled in your arms
The shadow becoming one

I watched your child at your breast
The outline of contentment and I felt
Engulfed by the beauty of it

I watched you and you didn't know
I was there
In the beginning in awe of what was to become
In the end for all the mourning that had to be done

Diane Whitman
Island Park, NY

The Present Moment

Now is not the time to take a break…
    think too much or hesitate.
Now is the time to be right here…
    this "present moment" is so dear.
The only time that really counts…
    or if at all much does amount.
The past is gone—just memories…
    like a blossom's scent upon the breeze.
Some things are cherished in the mind…
    other things best left behind.
The future is some have surely shown…
    something simply best unknown.
Prepare for it as best we may…
    but yet to come is this new day.
So heed! Right now right here is real…
    to enjoy it now is our best deal.
Try not to fret of what might come…
    or live in guilt of what is done.
We shouldn't fear, of this I'm sure…
    what lies beyond our future's door.
But the very most important time to "be"…
    is in this "present moment"
        can't you see!

Leon Truex
Jackson, NJ

To Serve

Today I pledge a new beginning,
to serve my fellow man
by speaking and doing what I believe is right
and lending a helping hand.

Some years ago my life was reckless
now, what difference does that make?
For I have given my life to God
a new me He did make.

As I plunge into giving service
someone always brings up my past
but yet I have no need to worry
because I'm free at last.

Yesterday has come and gone
to never, never return
yet today, tomorrow, will be yesterday
which make the inner heart yearn.

Now I'm serving in the highest office
which God's grace has put me there,
to praise Him and be a guiding light
and serve with loving care.

Selma Woods
Wyncote, PA

Restoration

How silently love begins
With a tiny spark, a glow within
The heart that's been broken,
Struggling to beat.
Love begins a steady rhythm
A life-glowing flow
A warmth that shields against
The cold, cold winds that blow.
Love, how can it be described?
Wild and racing, calm and serene,
A door that opens wide
To reveal a breathtaking scene.
More than an emotion
Higher than the heavens,
Deeper than the ocean.
The reality of perfection,
Blending breath and spirit.
Life, the result of creation
Let's be willing to truly live it,
To share it with others,
Who may also be broken
And need restoration.

Carol Stangle
Leechburg, PA

Hunter's/Fisherman's One Week Widow

I miss you in the morning
I miss you during the night
I miss you every moment
I long to hold you tight—

I jump into my jammies
And crawl into my lonely bed
I go to sleep remembering
All the little things you've said—

I wake up in the morning
And look at your empty pillow
My tears all come out heavy
Just like a weeping willow—

I drive the busy freeway
Thinking of you all the way
At least my job at the office
Helps me pass the day—

I'll do this Monday Tuesday
And of course the rest of the week
And then it will be Saturday
I'm almost at the peak

I'll drive the cabbie crazy
We don't want to be late
I'll meet that special person
We have a Saturday night date—

Audrey Kasper
Hacienda Heights, CA

My Printed Feedsack Skirt

My family large, the money low
I'll get some shoes before it snows
I love my friend's hand-me-downs
Thank you, Lord, for the hand-me-downs

Grandma as sweet as she can be
She left some printed feedsacks for me
With pretty spring flowered prints
I'd love a gathered flowered skirt

That printed feedsack, a skirt I'll make
Like the other girls at school wear
Some people looked, some people stared
But today I felt like a millionaire

Connie L. Chaplin
Wabash, IN

Life's Hands

The baby in the cradle
Reaching for its rattle,
Soft hands, tiny fingers
Caressing each small object.
Hands dimple with joy of life;
Not yet fearing fear;
Small, happy, young.
The man clutching the telephone pole;
Strong hands
Hardened from labor and work.
A train clatters by:
The hand grasps the pole, holding firmly;
Not smooth or dainty
But rough and dedicated.
Old hands tatting a doily;
Capable hands, now shaking with age.
Hands that lived through:
Joy, sorrow, fear, need.
Hands tired and ready for rest:
But hands still useful.

Norma Mercer
Fernbey, NV

God's Wonderful World

Consider the beautiful picture
Painted by God's hand
On the wide expanse,
of this great land.

The sky so blue,
the grass so green,
The host of multi-colored
flowers in between

The earth so brown
And clouds of white
In the background the sun
With the moon by night.

Fireworks of lightning,
Then the sun bursts through
And God paints a rainbow
of beautiful hue.

Sunsets ever changing,
sunrises always new
what more can I say,
Except, "God I Thank You."

Irene Lynn
Smithfield, PA

Exotic Dancer

If I were an exotic dancer how cool would that be.
I'd wear those skimpy clothes that barely cover me.
With six inch heels to lift me up long legs as you can see,
I'd swing from the pole so graceful and so true
Till you empty out your wallets and ask me when I'm through.
The black are glowing my outfit looks great
The music is blaring no time to escape.
The room is oh so smokey I cannot see his face
Thank God my shift is over it's time to be replaced.
You cannot have my number I'd like to be alone
God help me make my journey and take me safely home.

Darlene Yano
Diamond, OH

Poetry

Poetry is the sweet flow of words
that can express any feeling
Poetry comes from within you,
swirling around your brain
and through your fingertips
until it reaches the paper
Your poetry will never be the same
as someone else's
it is yours to bend
or twist
or twirl
or throw away
into the wind
and let someone else catch it
and be inspired
to write a poem
and let it go
so someone else will want to write a poem
and throw it away
so that one day,
the world will be filled with poets.

Jeanne M. Hathway
Silver Spring, MD

Will She Call Me Mama?

Here at my feet is a box of second-hand dolls,
Once deeply loved, washed, dressed, and fed
By little girls, playing at being mothers.
Now they are scruffy, dirty, naked, well-worn cast offs.
The soon-to-be little pretend mothers
Wait for that impish old stork, Santa Claus,
To leave the Cuddles, Bubbles, Thumbelina, Byelos, and Barbies
Beneath fashion designer Christmas trees.
One doll is missing both her arms; one's missing a leg.
Another has lost her hair much like a child sick from radiation.
Shall I deposit these defective effigies in my wastebasket?
Or will a needy child welcome and love
A maimed replica of herself?
A frilly bonnet may hide a hairless head.
These pitiful shapes with plastic birth defects,
Dried milk and crayola baby food on their faces,
With make-believe measles and bumps and bruises
On their bodies will be rehabilitated by grandmothers
Who have nothing else to do and who know that little girls
Still need dolls and that dolls still need little girls.
Christmas boxes raise existential questions to be answered on Christmas
morning.
Is a doll a doll, as the anthropologist might pose it? Will a little black girl
Clutch a frousled hair white doll to her breast and whisper, "I love you"?
What irony resides in acts of charity?

Juanita D. Sandford
Arkadelphia, AR

I am a retired professor of sociology and the author of "Poverty in the Land of Opportunity," a study of poverty in Arkansas. In addition to teaching, I was the coordinator of Woman's Studies at Henderson State University and served on the Governor's Commission on the status of woman. Other published works are "Being Poor in Arkansas" and "Woman's Liberation, the Church and Society," and chapters in books by other authors. In 1991 I was awarded the Doctor of Laws degree by Hendrix College, which each year gives the Juanita D. Sandford Social Justice Award to its outstanding graduate in Sociology.

D.J.M.

He's held our hands; he's watched us fall,
We could count on him through it all.
Father, Son, Husband, Brother,
His list continues on and on, but still his position could never be replaced
by another.
He's made our hearts grow with every simple grin,
And in our souls he will remain within.
None have known a man more comfortable in his shoes,
This character is going to be the hardest of them all to lose.
How do we start to move on, how do we part?
When his giant presence would calm our racing hearts.
When you think of him, please don't mourn for too long,
Remember his laughter and it will help to keep you strong.
He won't be forgotten, and forever live on,
Thank you for gracing us with so much life, Douglas Jon.

Sarah McClelland
Sandy, UT

Imagination

Under the sea, schools of tropical fish
entertain themselves by flipping and twirling in their show,

Up in the sky, birds soar above us as if guardians prepared to warn us about
upcoming trouble,

On the land, animals prowl about, darting after their prey,

But in my mind, things aren't always what they seem, and anything can happen
if you only believe,

For imagination is the best thing to me,
more important than the land, the sky, the sea

McCoy Allen
Cedar City, UT

I wrote this poem because I feel it reflects the way I see things. Looking through my eyes, I see in every person a special talent in them that no one else can do. Call it an ability! Whether it be seeing glimpses of the future, reading others minds, or just being able to put your thoughts and feelings on to a sheet of paper. I see my little brother daydreaming about what it would be like to have superpowers like Superman and Spiderman, when in reality, we all have supernatural powers inside of us. My goal is to make kids realize that writing a two-page report isn't just more work to do! It's a chance to find your superpower!

The One That Got Away

When I was young, so long ago,
I'd sit on Grampa's knee
And listen to his fishin' tales
Wide-eyed as I could be
And I can still remember
How he'd kinda' grin and say,
"The biggest one you ever saw
Was the one that got away!"
Well, time went on as time will do
And youth is gone so soon.
Now you'll find me fishin'
On most any afternoon.
Tryin' for a lunker bass
Or castin' for a trout.
I see'em in the water
But I seldom get'em out.
Then, all at once, I get a bite!
But I feel that leader snap.
And I realize that big one's
Gonna stay right where he's at.
But you know it's really worth it
When I think of gettin' gray
And I can tell my grandson on my knee
About the one that got away!!

Mike Shurtz
Saint George, UT

145

Fellowship

The runners have vanished from the road,
A coin, a broken twig, a toad.

They now count steps, when once 'twas miles'
But stay the course, and keep their smiles.

Age has taken the spring in their step,
A lumbering gait, an arduous trek.

Reflect and remember, no longer compete,
Age brings wisdom, a delectable treat.

The fellowship remains steadfast,
Bound by memories of good times past.

Bill Kaplan
Pomona, NY

The Only Key

Emotional puppets, dripping with feelings somebody else brought
Pointing your finger, skipping right over how it was I might have thought
Promises and pain, hand holding, change undisturbed
Practicing your pity on a crowd, your performance most absurd
I've heard every last word, last being the beginning tales and from now
on
Maddening this dangerous game—I wish my doubts could be gone
Bankrupt all your wit, care the way you brightened and baffled a room
Broken and lost, what you demand—do and don't, I can only assume
Distance of land and time, and further away now your mind
In between many questions—with no suitable answer to find
Every thought of you and joy—passionately my heart should fill
Can't imagine what's infected me, why my blood is so cold and still
Generously you pass me all the blame, minus any clues
Paying for what I have no idea, my grievous past dues
I should but can't break free from all that you do
Making me feel all of yours, as well as mine too
Hoping to rewrite until it's the last thing we see
You always had my heart never noticing—you had the only key

Sharri A. Gee
Defiance, OH

147

A Poem For Mimi and Linus

Mimi has a house!
Her flowers decorate it!
They make a rainbow!
Linus is her pal!
He travels on roller skates!
He visits Mimi!
They both grow flowers!
Some of them have shades of fall!
Some of them are blue!
Some have cherry shades!
Some of them glow with purple!
Some flowers are pink!
Flowers are their pals!
Together, they create bliss!
Flowers fill their hearts!
Linus is cheery!
He enjoys birthday parties!
His is coming up!
When his big day comes,
Mimi sings ''Happy Birthday!''
She gives him flowers!

Laraine Smith
Greencastle, IN

A Perfect Life

In the open or in a true secret
in my perfect life.
Enough to know myself better in 2009.
I can an the flames of desire and lead
to wrong conduct.
Is it because of the career job?
What are my own spiritual attributes?

So before I'm ready to focus on one particular
perfect life person,
How would I respond as a perfect life
spiritual woman.
Told to keep it a true secret about a perfect life
as a true Christian.

A perfect life there varies only with
the reasons and thus is safely ensconced
in the predictability of nature,
I swear that I wish to ease aside all
religious differences.
Please give my own reply to the accompanying
e-mail messenger.
This way I will learn humility and true perfect life career attitude.

Roberta J. Robinson
Akron, OH

149

I Want to Talk to Nana

It's been a long long time, since I talked to Nana Joan.
I guess I'll call her up on the telephone.
I can dial Nana's number, I heard it on TV.
I think it starts with 911, but all I heard was "EMILY!"

Mama was yelling, "Emily, EMILY."
"Put down that telephone, you've reached emergency!"
"What is your emergency?" I heard the lady say.
"I want to talk to Nana, can she come here today?"

"Please hang up your telephone, and do it right away!"
"This is only for emergencies and not for you to play!"
Then Mama reached the phone and stood me by the wall.
She apologized to the lady and quickly stopped the call.

I'll try again to call my Nana, she really is a peach!
"This is the overseas operator, who were you trying to reach?"
"I want to talk to Nana, but the lady's talking Dutch"
"I want to tell my Nana that I love her very much!"

Mary Gustafson
Waupun, WI

Cattails

Eye of newt and leg of toad,
Grinning black cats that cross your road
Be careful of the path you take
For hiss and growls are no mistake
Coming soon the signs are clear
All Hallows Eve will soon be here
The spirits of another day will soon be coming out to play
The sheepish grins and eerie sights are
Complimentary of the night
Who is it there beyond the tree? It could be one, it could be three!
For all that happens there is no doubt
The boogies they are all about
Thumps and bumps that fill the night
Will disappear in morning lights
Those that choose to find the source will be taken on another course
Be wary of your cat's meow for it may soon turn to howls
To fill the night on Halloween when leering jack o' lanterns beam
Soaring witches seen in flight, flying backwards in delight
Their choosing cats the best of show
No one knows which ones will go
Riding the brooms will be the sight
To court the moon on Halloween night
Meow

Linda L. Hulbert
Rice Lake, WI

Sheep Dog

I talk to my dog
and he talks to me
"bow wow" I don't think so
just "Let me in please"

He's smart as a whip
and knows all my moods
so I spoil him rotten
with play and good foods

I love him dearly
and it's plain to see
That he's my best friend
My sheep dog and me

Laurie Ross
Kilauea, HI

The Road

Driving on a lonely highway the blacktop glowing in the moonlight. The radio playing a sweet country song, windows down the crisp night air flows through.

With no destination is mind a run down shack comes to view. Getting out for a stretch, stumbling on a small stone "sweet child."

Wondering how you left this world, so young with much to do and see. Did you have blue eyes that sparkled with mischief? Did sickness take over your small body, leaving you frail and blue? Hoping that this was not true.

Getting back in the car, driving on that lonely highway with no destination in mind. Looking back seeing a glow on that small stone, with the radio playing a sweet country song.

Lisa Curtis
Jackson, NJ

Outside Window

As cold as death—as warmth embraced,
A wintry landscape shows its face.
A solemn hush—a crisp bright rush
Of quiet wind through sleepy brush.
There is a splendor here that softly falls
Like snowflakes down on slowly piling drifts;
And quiet beyond all depth reigns in the halls
Of wintry forest malls; hangs in the mists;
And contemplation hovers on the wings
Of the smallest birds left warbling in the trees
What you do not hear is most profound,
It's bluntly muted echoes now rebound,
Even the rays of the sun seem sparks of ice
Haloing a field that does entice
Toward an eternal majesty of silence
Beyond the graves of our most lofty goals.

S. P. Harrell
Louisville, KY

My Mother's Hands

Quietly sitting with her on her final day,
I can't believe Mom's passing away.
Slipping her hand gently into mine,
I look at them closely for what they remind.
Remind me of gentleness, kindness and love,
A Mother's guidance a gift from above
My Mother's hands they seldom did rest.
She strived so hard to just do her best.
The years went by swiftly and as I grew,
My mother's hands still guided me thru.
Wrinkled, transparent, aged now and worn,
I noticed the ring that she's always adorn.
The ring showing her love for her partner in life,
Memories of her being my father's wife.
I know how I'll miss their loving touch.
The grief that I'm feeling it hurts just so much.
Knowing they're slipping away now from me,
The familiar form I'll no longer see.
Still her hands presence I'll always find,
Memories of hands loving and kind.
Remembering hands folded in prayer,
Within a faith in God we did share.
Someday I'm hoping hands open wide,
In Heaven she'll welcome me back by her side.

Paula Chadwick
Stetson, ME

155

Is It?

If it is inner, it is
like living inside a red emotion
surrounded by the upside-down punchbowl
of a strawberry-lemonade sky

If it is inner, it is like
the purple bubbling, swirling
out of the dirt, out of the deep brown
smelling of the warmth of the earth

If it is inner, then it is
as true as my soul, that stands
on the cloudy white between the realism of land
and the green vapors of the ideal sky

If it is inner, as it always seems
then all your words are blue
cracking open like little birds' eggs
with the singing that makes them real

If it is inner, as it is
when the seeds of wildflowers bloom
when our future is more than a passing yellow
and it is not of me, nor of you, but of us
and it's true.

Jenni Miller
Chico, CA

A Spirit of Change

.do you feel a change coming
.a feeling that can't compare
.a Tsunami's in the rising of the sun
.I see it in the atmosphere
.the plates in the earth have snapped back
.they are out of their respective place
.the loss of their alignment
.has set the time a few seconds short the pace
.and washed out the old face
.there are changes in the governments
.almost seems like a new world emerged
.a mighty rushing wind has come
.and has done its task
.to equalize a set of systems
.that were biased in the past
.all over the world
.journeys are gonna change
.election results are essential
.and so to everything must change
.Barack Obama, a man
.with no single solitary heritage
.a person with a mandate
.the face of the American flag.

Lorraine Joyner-Gregg
New York, NY

The Beauty of the Universe

The sun a sign of God's warm love
shines its rays from the heavens above.

It brightens my spirit by beginning each new day
and sheds its light and warmth along my way.

It touches me so gently on every side
as it stretches for miles so far and wide.

Reflecting on the waters; it mirrors
the beauty of God's face
Passing over land and the sea; reaches
each and every place.

As its brightness fades into darkness and
dusk sets on the earth
it slowly dims and hides until the dawn
calls it to new birth.

The rolling clouds passing quickly, the gentle
breeze of the bowing trees
Whisper clearly to me, "See, I'm right here
in all of these."

The heavens, earth, sea, trees and plants
come forth at his command
For the beauty of the universe is the
handiwork of God's creating hand.

Sister Karen Buco
Pittsburg, PA

Weather

The weather is unpredictable at times,
So I know not to try to predict all the time.
I am a kind person who knows the weather,
But the earth air is like a feather in weather.
I want to give a word of kindness
That the weather is not kind to me but I can give acts of kindness.
So next time it is brutal give acts of kindness to your fellowman.
There is good in everyone so let's make it good for everyone
Now and forever. Amen.

Brian Troup
Indiana, PA

Untitled

My heart fell from my chest, to my
feet because those words "I hate you"
came from your mouth. These words are
tears that fell from my eyes as I
looked at you. While my heart
dropped to the ground, you held me
down when you knocked me over and I
couldn't get up. You let me lie there
in pain of loneliness in my mind,
and now I'm fading away out of this
in-closed world of mine, and my time
is finally up, it's time for me to
Say "Goodbye."

Chaylea Goodyear
Thomasville, NC

159

Call Me Sam

Sam is not short for Samantha or Samuel
I am neither boy nor girl—I am a person

I am independent
I am silly

I am fun-loving
I am a friend to everyone, and I don't know an enemy

I feel joy and pain
I hurt, I need

I have hopes and dreams
I cry when I'm sad and laugh when I'm happy

I live, laugh and love
I am like no other

You can call me S.A.M. because I'm Simply Amazing Me
Sam I am

Beverly Smith
Franklin, IN

Romeo and Juliet

Will you be the Romeo to my Juliet?
Can you love me forever with no regret?
Can you stay in love with me forever?
A love for you is what I sever.
Regret nothing, do your best.
You will become different from the rest
It has always been you that I adore
I cannot deny my love anymore.
Give me a chance I beg you please.
I cry for forgiveness on my knees.
I will do anything, even die.
As long as you stay by my side.
Hear my plead, sing my song.
You're the one I wanted all along.
There is no other like you
These are things that are true
Ask anyone, asked around
My heart was shackled and bound
A kiss so tender and sweet
Just like the moment we meet
Not much known, nor does it matter
With my words, I hope to flatter.
I will see you in heaven, I promise this.
I will leave you with one final kiss.

Teri L. Smith
Lake Katrine, NY

Heart of Gold

Eyes of brown
Heart of gold
For you are forever a part of my soul

You bring me smiles of love
Joys of laughter
Touched by your heart of gold

Your strong broad arms hold me tight
From break of dawn to fall of night

My heart will treasure you
From day to night,
For your love is might

When I sleep I pray the night to keep you safe
Till I awake and see your smiling face

With your arms wrapped in my embrace
Like a bow we are in the perfect place

We shall forever have and to hold
For your heart of gold has touched my soul.

Julie R. Barnes
Avon, IN

Love and Aging

Wrinkles appear.
Unseen,
as vision dims.

Music plays.
Unheard,
as hearing fails.

Dinner cools.
Uneaten,
as hunger wanes.

Together we sit.
Patient,
hand in hand

Waiting.

Marguerite Sowaal
Lucerne Valley, CA

It's no fun to anticipate watching your mate deteriorate (and what's worse put it in verse). These poems were written to express my feelings while tending to my husband's Alzheimer's condition.

To Baby

This is a story from daddy to you,
It all started out with a dot that turned blue.
Your mom and I got married in May,
And you were in the making the very next day.
It was just a short time after that,
Mommy complained that she was too fat.
I took pictures of her belly as she grew,
And grew and grew to make room for you.
Your mom was a champ and never got sick,
But farted and peed like a beer-bellied hick.
Choosing your name was an arduous chore,
It was Paige then Brianne, Mickey, Taylor and more.
Everyone said you were going to be late.
But Mommy was praying for an early due date.
We enrolled you in school even before you were born,
To teach you how to get out without leaving Mom worn.
You learned well and Mom learned fast.
She'd scream, "Epidural, and it damn better last."
Now, there's just one short month to go,
So until then, curl up and then shift into low.
Your Mom and I are going to be so happy,
Meanwhile, take your time baking, but
"Hey, make it snappy."

Russ Scarborough
Surprise, AZ

164

My Baby

I look out my window
As I watch you stare
Towards nature's beauty
And the birds in the air

A coffee cup steams
With the morning sun
I know right then
Today will be fun

What a delight it is
For me to seek
A moment in time
To kiss your cheek

Good morning my
Woman of Paradise
Some breakfast soon
Would really be nice

Edward R. Fritz
Bluemont, VA

Santa's Joy of Christmas

Santa comes a greetin'
Little boys and girls
Jingle bells a jinglin'
Round the snow it swirls

Jim Dandy and Candy
Friends of Santa, too
Care about Rudolph
As all reindeer do
Santa's joy of Christmas
To bellow out ho! ho! ho!
A Merry, Merry Christmas
A joyous year aglow

Edward Baubie
Harper Woods, MI

Untitled

Ah there was a time
When the summer flood
Leaped freely in my veins
And I'd rise from the pillow
From night dark sleep
To seize the morning's reins
With eager joy in all my parts
The day a lover and I its mate
Aglow in the endless strength of youth

Now old eyes see
Where young eyes turned away
And strength gives out
In struggles with the day
Knowing each morning could be the last
Yet still that thrill of a voyage past
Time to what wonders lie in store
Beyond that final shaded door
Where answers at last reveal all truth

William Evers
Long Beach, NY

A Poem

Wilderness is the natural untouched lands, with its majestic beauty and scenic aura.
It's the flight of the eagle as it passes by the flowing trout stream.
It is the call of the wolf pack on a cold winter's night.
The sound of the whip-poor will on a warm summer evening.
The call of the morning dove first thing in the morning.
The cool smell of the fir tree's along the mountain road, just after a summer rain.
The tree frogs chirping in another mating season.
Early morning gobble of the wild turkey, strutting around for the waiting hens.
The return of the humming bird as it signals in yet another spring.
The salmon run on an early fall day just as the leaves are turning.
This is what wilderness and outdoors means to me.

Jimmy Graham
Columbia, SC

The Loner

Never trusting
Always wanting a friend
Never drawing any near
Keeping to himself
Unable to feel connected
Always wanting to fit in
Looking in from outside
Observing how others live
Are they truly happy
He wonders
Are they content with their friends
Loner wishes he could trust
Wishes he could blend
Wanting things like others have
Family
No one wants him
No invitations in from the cold
Loner has no escape from Winters fury
His cold, cold heart paralyzes his soul
Always the observer
Never a participator
Never growing as a person
Zombie
Death of a mind

Carlton Rollins
New Sharon, ME

Shade Of the Maple Tree

I can still feel the breeze of the wind.
Sitting in the straight back chairs,
The leaves waving with the flow of wind.
Bringing a refreshing breeze of air.

I wish I could go back under the tree.
It would renew my spirits
Just to breathe the fresh air.

The maple tree had to be cut down,
And there was nothing like its shade.
Family gatherings won't be the same.
We won't be gathering there anymore.

Oh, if you ever have a chance,
To sit under a maple tree,
Sit and refresh your spirit.
It's the most refreshing experience,
Sitting in the shade of a maple tree.

Aline Burton
London, KY

Pathways

My friend of long years past
You walk the pathways of my mind
Your guidance will forever last
Gently showing the pathways so kind

Your presence is like a cool breeze
Soft words spoken in my dreams
Reminding me of a treasured past
Your guiding light continuous gleams

Things we shared and talks we had
Pointing a way to an easier path
Teaching, sharing of experience
Remembering keeps me to the truer way

We knew and loved a stronger light
One who traveled a more dangerous road
He counseled this world with all his might
To Golgotha he carried his load

I remember your loving touch and strong hands
So much more than just a show of might
A friendship that forever stands
My lost companion and guiding light

Showing the way to achieve manhood
A truer friend I've never had
Making traditions of all that is good
I love you and miss you, My Dad

Danny C. Evans
O'Brien, FL

171

It's Time

It's time to set free our caged, restless demons.
But our cages are sometimes filled with tranquil doves.
It's time to open our tired weary eyes.
But, sometimes the bright light is blinding.
It's time to examine and analyze our earlier lives.
But, lack of motivation prevents any rememberings.
It's time to do away with contempt and prejudices.
But, the dents in our souls are deeply rooted.
It's time to accept our deep inherited faith.
But, sometimes distrust and disbelief will not dissolve.
It's time to unlock our life-sustaining hearts.
But, being solely contingent is dangerous.
It's time to discuss our differences and disagreements.
But, open minds and compatibility are rare commodities
It's time to take stock of our privileges and fortunes.
But, we are unable to recall or reexamine our assets.
It's time to rid our intellect of outmoded and hostile ideologies
But, ego and self-importance keep offering up road blocks.
It's time to cultivate friendships and acquaintances.
But, some people have become withdrawn and unsociable.
It's time to face our obstacles, hazards and risks.
But, standing tall is difficult and complicated.
It's time to shine light on shameful, hidden agendas.
But, the underestimated wattage may not be sufficient.

Dick Burton
Lincoln, NE

Death Came

Death came one night
and claimed my son;
without a warning
he was gone.

My hollow heart cries out,
my tears flow free.
I ask, "Oh, God,
why him, why not me?"

I lie in the dark
in infinite numbness and pain;
knowing in this life,
I will never see him again.

I so miss his smile,
the twinkle in his eye, his gentle ways,
so afraid I will forget,
as the hours turn into days.

He will live forever in my heart,
that is one thing I do know.
And I expect to see his smile again,
when it is my time to go.

I know he is with God
with angels all around;
no pain, no fear or ridicule
complete joy he has found.

Toni Tunmer
Tipton, IN

Somewhere over the Rainbow

"Somewhere Over the Rainbow"
Has always been my favorite song,
Since I was 12 years old
And heard it, I would sing along.

When I grew up and married,
Each child I gave birth to would hear
Me sing it as a lullaby
As bedtime would draw near,

I don't really know what it is,
Just the words or the melody,
Or maybe it is the word "Rainbow"
That means so much to me.

It reminds me of God's Promise,
He gave to Noah and his family then
He kept them safe in the Ark Noah built
And promised never to flood the earth again.

So don't be sad when it's stormy
Because sunshine will soon break through
And "Somewhere Over The Rainbow"
A new day is dawning for you

Doreen A. Stirm
Independence, IA

Orange and Green

Orange is our music teacher singing a song
When our whole class is singing along
Orange is words, in a poem, that rhyme
Orange is the favorite color of mine
Orange is fire,
The rage you feel when someone calls you a liar
Orange is the kind words that you say
It's the flaming torch on Olympic Day
Orange is the juicy fruit that you eat for snack
Orange is the knowledge that some people lack
Orange is the full moon and pumpkins on Halloween night
Orange is the color of Sunny Delight
It's the color of my favorite vest
And last of all, the color I like best

Green is the grass glistening with dew,
Raindrops on leaves, and rose petals too
Green is a pear, bursting with juice
Green is a thick forest of pine trees and spruce
Green is like jealousy and eyes full of spite
Green is like beauty, shimmering so bright
Green is the very start of spring, when color just begins to show
And small patches of weeds emerging from under the snow

Rachael Friedman
Evans, GA

175

Mike

Little kindnesses never gendered,
Good intentions un-matured.
Present state of mind is shattered,
All of this now sadly blurred.

Notes of cheer I could have written,
Well placed words I could have said,
Undone deeds—my heart is smitten,
I just learned a friend is dead.

Joseph E. Bloomer
Springfield, MO

Journey

Wrap yourself in this prayer shawl
And join me on a journey
Of stitches and rows in wool;
This journey is entwined
At every twist and turn
With prayer, caring and warmth for thee;
Therefore, wrap yourself in this shawl,
And join me in this prayer journey.

Janet L. Routson
Amarillo, TX

176

American Pride

The sun still shines
The birds still sing
To be an American is such a wonderful thing!
Our hearts still heavy
Tears still fall
United as one, WE ALL STAND TALL!
Our nation is strong our will is too
With family and friends at our side, there is nothing we can't get through
The battles upon us
The lines have been drawn
Good vs. Evil the fight is on
Never lose faith, fill your hearts with pride and never forget those that
died
WE WILL NEVER FORGET!

Manny Vitale
Roseville, MI

177

Images

Are both of you a Sunday in this year's fall,
Calling your families to witness solemn vows
Not in church, but in your fragrant garden small
Where brilliant smiles do wreath your brows?
Is it images that make this moment stand out so?
Let's list them, there's enough to catch a rhyme
Two faces on airport monitors, faces all aglow,
Years and years of moments standing fast in time;

Rescue Papa at the Irish Soldier's library video
Barf terribly at the kitchen's horrid bacon smell
Bring forth the one, the only, the first, the show
And then a second, unlike the first, a child to tell
The ages, "I know exactly what I will do now."
The four of them, blessed happy lives, bow.

Quentin Baker
Milpitas, CA

If I Could Have One Wish

If I could have one wish, I'd wish for all to see,
The happiness and joy our families should bring.
Smiling faces, children playing, so happy and carefree;
But that's not always how it goes...at least it's not for me.

War torn countries with shattered lives, no place to call your own.
No place for children to laugh and play, no place to call home.
Only cries for peace and hope, yearning to be free,
What the future holds for man, only God can see.

Broken homes and tears of pain, hearts that want to heal;
Seek for peace and harmony, against man's will.

I have no words of comfort, only pain and fear.
We teach our children hate, not love...
That's why we all shed tears.

So if I could have one wish today,
It would be for us to be,
A united worldwide family with peace and harmony.

Carol L. Cocke
Clarendon, TX

It's Tough Getting Old

I have such an interesting social life
It really is a crime,
I go to see my doctor,
Every Friday morn at nine,

He takes four vials of blood each time
Which makes me very squeamish
And then he turns around and tells me;
"You know, you are anemic?"
He took some X-rays of my hip
And found that I am lacking
The cartilage between the bones
And that's why they are "clacking."

My thyroid's low my blood pressure's high,
And sometimes 'I wish that I could die,'
But that is due to my depression
And to my broken-heart condition.
Then on Tuesdays, I go to see
My ophthalmologist, who's far from "free."
He tells me I have degeneration
And cataracts starting THEIR formation.

I slowly breathe a great big sigh
.And think "Guess I'll live until I die."
After all, I'm already seventy-two,
With twenty-four grandchildren in my "crew."

Joyce Runyan
Turlock, CA

Untitled

On a cold December day
Our beloved Pupper passed away
Always faithful to the end
She was a very special friend
Running out to meet us
She was always there to greet us
Coming home from work or play
Waiting for our return all day
Getting older she grew weak
Unable to stand on her back feet
We had to say our last good-bye
It's hard to watch an old friend die
We will not soon forget her
She was ours for years your see
If there is a doggie heaven
I know exactly where she will be

MacCoy Johnson
Birnamwood, WI

There Is a Place Waiting for Me

There is a place waiting for me
Where the air is crisp and clean
Where the sky is a beautiful blue
Where the sun shines through to me

There is a place waiting for me
Where the birds can sing their songs
Where the water flows along its bumpy path
Where the animals are free to roam

There is a place waiting for me
Where sadness and strife are forgotten
Where sickness and death are behind us
Where love and joy will never leave us

There is a place waiting for me
Where life is nothing but a beautiful dream
Where everyone is free to come and go
Where dreams are made but not forgotten

There is a place waiting for me
Where all my dreams can come true
Where love will always be with me
Where is this wonderful place? "In you."

Eugene P. MacArthur
Gulfport, FL

Seasons

I love spring and summer
They're my favorite time of year.
With all the outside work to be done,
My husband's such a dear.

Then we come to fall,
it's football season,
And my wonderful guy is gone.
So here I go,
I'm on my own;
I'll have to rake the lawn.

Then basketball must come around
And he's tied up with that.
Till March is over, he's not my guy
He's just a darned old rat.

Thank goodness he's not into baseball.

Mary L. Mudrick
Weirton, WV

Happy Father's Day, Dad

Father's day is coming and I am feeling kinda sad,
because I don't remember a whole lot about my dad.
I may not have a lot of them, but let me make one thing clear,
the memories I do have of him, I hold very dear.

I remember when we would play sports out in the backyard.
We'd toss a ball back and forth, sometimes pretty hard.
We played in the yard so often, we wore dirt holes in the grass,
because we'd be playing baseball or I'd go out for a pass.

The one memory that I have that keeps running through my head,
is my dad was really nice and kept his family fed.
Or when he came home and took his smokes out from where he had
them hid.
He said, "I'm going to quit smoking," and you know by God he did.

Since he was young my dad's hair was gray, and please excuse the pun,
but it's this hair raising trait he passed on to his only son.
I got his sense of humor, the kind that makes you slap your knee.
But since I don't get a lot of laughs, I guess the joke's on me.

Dad, if you are listening to me, in Heaven up above,
please know that I still think of you, and send you all my love.
I wrote this poem to let you know what a good job I thought you had
done.
And to thank you for all your love, I'm signing it, Bob, your son.

Robert Ford
McHenry, IL

184

History Of the S.U.V.

First came the horse & buggy
when I was but a child,
we could travel down country lanes
except if the horse was wild.

The covered wagon was okay,
convenient at most,
but can you just imagine
traveling in one coast to coast.

The Model T next invented
which we thought was grand,
when you chose to make a turn
you would signal with your hand.

Ford Motor Company got the idea
for a shiny new car,
roads were bad way back then
so we didn't travel far.

We then needed a place to stay
when away from home at night,
so an R.V. next in line
which we thought all right.

Now you brag about you S.U.V.
and smooth roads all a glaze,
but at my age you should know
I'd go back to the 'good ole days!'

Winnie Sweatt
Amarillo, TX

Friendship

Friendship comes on angel's wings
To soothe an aching heart
It's in the simple little things—
A smile can make it start.
It fills our lives with so much joy
And joins our hearts in love,
It understands our deepest needs,
A gift from God above.
It endures the test of time
And lasts our whole life through.
I'm thankful for this gift I have
Because, my friend, it's you!

Richard Lemke
Greer, SC

The Smile

Folks say that love is a one way street,
But that all depends on just who you meet.
If you give them a smile and get one back,
Then it seems to me, that you're on the right track.
A kind word with a "How are you today?"
Will ease their burden and brighten their way.
A smile is much easier than a horrid old frown,
Who knows what that old grouch has been through.
Maybe it would have done the same to me and to you.
So put your best foot forward and do what you can,
Because there is surely some good in every man.
So go forth, my darling, and spread cheer and love,
And you will receive blessings from above.

Phyllis Fifer
Sierra Vista, AZ

Paula

Bright and cheerful, perpetual motion,
Thoughtful, courageous, charged with emotion.
Full of charisma, sometimes she sees red,
Fully alive, from her toes to her head.

Devoted, enchanting, the queen of the hill,
Moved by the Spirit, the Mrs. of Bill.
Mother and wife, as a friend there's none better.
She delights in a flower or in reading a letter.
God-fearing woman, a hard worker for sure,
Never too tired to do one more chore.
Concerned about those less fortunate than her,
Dreams of Tom Selleck and a coat made of fur.
There when you need her, never far away,
Sharing a smile and the right thing to say.
She's one in a million, none can compare.
The world's so much better cause of this lady fair.

Ted Zeunges
Woodbridge, VA

Icicle

The beauty of sharpness
And transparency,
Pure and frigid stillness

Formed, drop on drop
Running water stopped
Delayed in its fall

Only to decorate
Until sun's heat
Cuts it down.

Carolyn G. Goodridge
Windsor Locks, CT

Life

Life, a living being a man, woman and child
God breathed into man nostrils the breath of life
and became a living soul
Life, trail, hardship, joy and happiness.
Life, work, pain, rest and comfort.
Life, war, hate, peace and love.
Life, sickness, sorrow, well and exalted.
Life, poor, worry, rich and fine.
Life, failure, loss, greatness and gain.
Life, to live, to die.

Preston Evans
Jackson, MS

Welcome the Sunshine

The sun is trying to break through
Those heavy clouds that are hovering.
Then our spirits drop so low
We feel we're beyond recovering.

That's when all the bad things in our lives
Open up in our memory—
Things that we had hidden
For absolutely none to see.

Each time that they appear
They seem to grow bigger in size,
They almost consume us
Until we realize

It is the darkness of the day
That makes us sad and blue.
Even the future is bleak,
And we know that that's not true.

But when the dark clouds move on
And the sunshine comes shining through,
Our good spirits now take over
And again allow us to do

All the nice things we can do.
When the sun is shining bright,
It makes such a difference
For our spirits when it's light.

Marie Sitzenkopf
Easton, MD

The Final Storm

A single rose stands aged and sick.
Her long thin stem arched over
And her fragile buds are wilting away.
She once was a fresh-bloomed blossom
With a sturdy stem and blush petals.
Her fragrance was a sweet perfume that filled the air.
The bumble bees would hum while collecting pollen
From her appealing bloom.

But now an unpredictable disease drifts through her veins.
Depressing clouds align like a funeral procession
As they roll over the distraught garden.
Rain pours, thunder roars and lightning begins to strike.
Her elderly roots struggle to consume the rain
That trickles off her shriveled rose petals
Like tears streaming down an old woman's wrinkled face.

The young blossoms come to a defeating silence
While they pray for her endurance.
But as forceful winds blow strong
Her delicate petals gently fall to the tranquil soil.
The lifeless body of a once beautiful Rose
Now quietly lies in a puddle of bittersweet rain.

Janelle Bollinger
Niles, OH

Welcome To My Hell

Welcome to my hell
your soul I will devour
gnashing teeth draw closer
to crush you with their power
The enemy sits beside you
his presence seems sincere
he deceives you with the lies
he whispers in you ear
gather up your forces
every able bodied soul
gather up your forces
begin the death bell toll
I will walk beside you
until the very end
where soon you will discover
I'm truly not your friend
people gather round
to say their last farewell
I alone am waiting
welcome to my hell

Debbie Fredrick
Lincoln, NE

Twins

There were twins both fair and bright,
Who sojourned always with peaceful night.

Sleep first recognized the bliss in dark,
And in so many mortal thoughts would strum his silver harp.

Death too was pacified with the distant stars,
And would come to those with burdens to relieve their heavy hearts.

Dusk became a happy time,
From whence the concern and care of humans left with lidded eyes.

No cloak but that of darkness, no veil but that of night,
Sleep and death are more deliverance than violent passions or evil
crimes.

In sleep there is such kindness, bed and pillow aside,
He offers such freedom in the diversion and asylum of mind.

And death—he is no villain, yet will be welcomed by none,
Ashen faces greet him, and wearied souls act as company to he who is
alone.

Such easy transport—to ferry the mind and dreams,
And pale night gowns litter the sky with the canopy of solace in death
and sleep.

Laura E. Matera
Columbia, MO

Route of Little Resistance

Beneath the brush of your wing
inside the thin muscle of your knowing
I open my gray coat.
Rain steady thru fine breath
like a curtain fluttering across the
shoulder of this room
here is a wish never quite the same, a
feather wrinkling in the womb of my mother.
You could ride your blue breath
into the last meadows of my secret
as if you believe we might soon tell
each other everything.
Dent ground as hard as flesh down here
I am small enough to lean so close.
A bird staring through the storm
might forget its name and
whisper love to the naked gravity
of our falling . . .

Richard Inman
Greenville, SC

I Am From

I am from a Mexican family,
Growing from generation to generation.
I am from an Indian tribe,
Dancing in the sparkling sky.
Spinning around the fire in the moonlight.
I am from a dream catcher flying back and forth
in the sparkling light trying to catch your dreams.
I am from a sparkler,
jumping and spinning in the foggy smoke
of the Fourth of July excitement.
I am from the sketches of three generations,
the gift of talent I am wishing to pass on.
I am from the ups and down of a roller coaster,
spinning in different directions.
I am from the seed of a flower, blowing in the spring wind,
waiting to find my place, in this free-spirited world.
I am from the cuts and bruises of my loving brothers,
Me wishing for a sister and now having my wish come true,
enjoying the giggles and laughter and teaching and preparing of all the
excitement that lies ahead of her in the future.
I am from four walls that were once broken,
But now put back together and adding four more.
I am from a pebbled rock, in my quiet, dead neighborhood,
watching everyone pass by without noticing me.

Alyssa Melchor
Yuba City, CA

Well I'm 13 years old and I have two brothers and one sister. I am the oldest kid in my family. And the thing that inspired me to write this poem was when I was younger my parents divorced and my mom re-married, and my dad had a girlfriend and had my little sister. So I was going through a lot of trouble back then, and I needed to know who I really was. The poem inspired me to look ahead and follow my dreams and don't worry about stuff that happened in the past.

Just Because I Care

Because I care, I want to know what's going on.
Please tell me baby, so I can right the wrong.
Because I care, as well as understand,
You need someone to lean on and who'll give a helping hand.
Because I care, I feel your sorrow.
And it makes me wish I could fix the problem.
Because I care, I want to shower you with gifts.
So close your eyes and make a wish.
Because I care, I will cater to you.
Even though sometimes, I'm not in the mood.
I'll do all these things, not because of some silly dare.
I'll do them simply …
Just because I care.

LaKeisha Brown
Taylor, MI

My Beautiful Trailmate

I love my trail mate.
She is a beautiful woman;
she gave me an oriental Goddess
of mercy and compassion.

I love to listen to her,
I remember what she said;
I keep her talk in my heart,
I learn to be her trail mate.

She adorns the desert trail,
she blends with beautiful nature;
with her beautiful singing voice
she enjoys to sing what she loves.

She enjoys to climb the hill,
and she feels healthy and happy;
she breathes deep as she walks,
and her beautiful name is Cathryn.

She is happy when the air is clean,
and the mountains look so lovely;
she stops to admire friendly nature,
and the sunshine makes her smile.

She loves the animals and birds,
and she walks in front of me;
she enjoys to be her precious self,
and she is grateful to be free.

Carlos Vanegas
Tucson, AZ

The Single Rose

The beauty of a single rose in itself is truth;
Its stem symbolizes growth, its delicate petals our fragile youth.

Plucked from the bush that harbors it the rose will surely perish;
In the time allowed my rose I've learned to cherish.

I nurture it with fluids and carefully snip its stem;
Enabling the single rose to drink in life again.

Eventually my rose will die, its petals wilt and fall;
But at least I've the satisfaction I've given it my all.

When my rose has withered, another I shall pick;
And so continues the story, and on and on the clock of life shall tick.

Jana S. Maron
Peoria, AZ

Life's Journey

On the journey through life we
Try to walk between the raindrops
This is our goal
To give and forgive is
Written on our soul
On this journey we hope
To be loved and to love
Hoping what we do will
Be approved from above
The journey we are on
Takes many years
It will teach us to be brave
And to face our fears
To help and to be helped
Is a special thing
And that honor and hope
We can always bring
Throughout your lives keep
These thoughts in mind
Then life to you will be sweet and kind

Ronald Feil
Sacramento, CA

Economic Fall

Staggering job loss
Has come at a cost
To the state of the union today
Only celebrities
Can spend as they please
On cars and foreclosed property

Corporate corruption
Leads to destruction
Like Halloween treats to decay
More banks will fold
Economists foretold
Leaving accounts empty payday

Airport screenings
Cold and demeaning
Send passengers safe on their way
Or so they assert,
Avoiding high alert
When amber's the color of the day

Consumer confidence continues to plummet
After each press conference and summit
As politicians proclaim and make hay
Winter wind chills
Raising heat bills
Where is global warming as scientists say?

Amy Drake
Columbus, OH

Amy Drake holds a B.A. from Ohio Dominican University where she is pursuing a master's degree in liberal studies. Amy has worked in communications for a large corporation and written on a freelance basis since 2003. Amy is also a professional speaker. In 2008 Amy was awarded the International Association of Business Communicators' Silver Quill Award of Excellence for online writing. Amy's education includes programs at Cambridge University, U.K. and Reed Hall, Paris, France. Amy is a member of IABC and serves on the board of the English Speaking Union. Amy is married to Dr. Miles E. Drake, Jr., a neurologist and opera expert.

The Days I Will Always Remember

I remember that day,
the day that was placed in the middle of May
That day was the first day of our friendship.
The images will never go away, of our very first
Spring trip.

I remember that day,
the day that you told me all you had to say.
The day that I should've given its value.
The words left unspoken were "I love you."

I remember that day,
the day that you were taken away.
That day will be etched in my mind and heart forever.
The image of your face in that casket will fade from me never.

Synclaire Land
Aurora, IN

Driving to Ventura

Red, purple and white oleanders line the asphalt freeway
Golden brown hills roll off to infinity
Caution wide turns
Brown whiskers of dead shrubs against the yellow ochre of the hills
Silver water tower whose pipe leads down, hugging the ground
Red tile roofs of the houses on the edge of the mountain
Merge left
Green golf course with erratic spots of moving white
Tall flag billowing, trailing it's frayed edges
Exit 30 MPH

Barb White
West Hills, CA

Stillness

Birdsong silenced,
Fireflies blink
Muted moonlight,
Shadows indistinct.
Sweet scent
Of summer night
Our world
On hold.

Nancy Flanagan
Oshkosh, WI

Preconscious

the bad reception of hours
transplants a green aura
onto a mind that I
always already
loved
and the mile
between your chin and my gaze
where your smile should be

words travel dimensions
and stop short
in a smoky room
where I cannot hear
for all the color
and your unbroken lines
broken
make word condensation
on my glass

I shiver at the brush
of lips
almost felt
but unknown
until I am better prepared

Susan Motschenbacher
Troy, MI

My Favorite Brother

My favorite love is my brother,
I'll tell you now, there is no other.
Everybody knew before too long,
When he was born, there was something wrong.
He didn't act as other little boys,
And wouldn't even play with toys.
The doctors said his brain didn't grow,
When we asked why? They didn't know.
Things were never really right.
Because he couldn't read or write.
His heart is always filled with love,
He's like a little turtle dove.
I guess I'll never ever see,
Why the good Lord let it be,
This is why he's my favorite brother,
And there will never ever be another.

Winifred J. Love
Abington, MA

I am the fourth child of twelve children. All my life I loved writing poetry, short stories, and always kept a diary. The eleventh of the twelve was born retarded. He was special to us all. I decided to write the poem about him. He couldn't read or write. He was like a six year old, sweet and innocent. Since I've written this poem, my dear brother passed away. He was forty-eight years old. We all miss him very much. This poem is in his honor.

In Loving Memory

Please do not grieve
My loved ones!
You all have made me happy
And I shall love you always,
Here in Heaven as with you on earth!

Why cry my demise,
When death has ended all sorrows?
What joy to contemplate my God
And confide in Him
All of your secret longings!

If you really loved me,
Pray often, and remember me.
Always remain united
And keep your faith
In our great Lord and Savior!

Do not grieve me,
My most dearly beloved.
Always remember that one day
We all shall be reunited
Together with our Lord and God Almighty!

Joyceline Huennekens
Weaverville, NC

1-800 Line to God

Storms come through our lives
There is a reason for all things
The stronger the storm
The more prepared for what life brings

Lightning lights up the sky
Leaving us with fear
But only for a short time
We know that God is near

The power line to God
No storm can tear apart
The knowledge of his love
Is securely bounded in my heart

I have a 1-800 Number to God
I know He is always there
He is always listening
To my every prayer

He knows what is best for me
It was planned before I came
With all my heart I will trust Him
I will praise His Holy Name.

Janie L. Bellomy
Arlington, TX

I am a mother of three married sons, four granddaughters, two grandsons, and one great grandson. I started writing poetry many years ago. My sister-in-law, who was dying with cancer, called me one day and asked if I would write a poem titled "1-800-Line to God." I told her it might be awhile in order for me to compose it. Right after I hung up the phone I was blessed and inspired with the words of the poem. I called her back and read it to her and she was surprised, amazed, and delighted than I had written it so quickly.

My Twin

You'll never know that you're my hero
My dear brother
You came home from Nam
and said "leave me alone"
And after all these years, my dear,
how you still suffer
Especially for your brothers
who didn't make it home
But my brother, I have never
Known a better man
And around you, oh how Jesus' light glows
And even after our sweet Lord has called you home
"Hero" is how you will be known

Dee Powell
Elkins, WV

Red

Red is like the blood from skin.
Red is like a fireman just coming in from an emergency.
Red is like the houses all around the community.

Red is like a beanbag we could share for you and me.
Red tastes like an apple that I eat at home.
Red smells like red sauce without being known.

Red sounds like a fire truck that just drove by.
Red feels like fire that is about to die.
Red looks like lips that you get on a kiss.
Red is like the jeans I tried on in a store.
Red tastes like a cherry, and so much more.

Red makes rubies feel warm and inviting.
Red is so exciting.

Tiffany Lewis
Brooklyn, NY

I'm Tiffany Lewis. I am 14 years old and in the 9th grade. I go to school at Frederick Douglas Academy VII High School. I have two brothers, Lennon and Quincy. My parents are Lorraine and George Lewis. What inspired me to write my poem is my wanting to show others what it means to me (the color red).

Meeting Room

There is a place I want you to meet me
It's a place where there is no tomorrow
A place where time is non existent, and ruled by memories
Where pain stands still and yields to happiness
Please come and find me here, it's called the meeting room
It's here where I'll find you pleasantly trapped within my dreams
Born again in the innocence of my spirit, the purity of my heart
Where your inner light shines as brightly as you would have it
Please meet me here, where you are cherished
The place where we both become open and reveal our vulnerabilities
Where we have no shame, only love; no secrets, only truths;
and no fears, only possibilities
Where hope truly does spring eternal
In this place enchanted where the things of fairy tales are made
Yes, just meet me here, my love, where I am yours, and I'll love you
Forever.

Tawnya Randle-Hedspeth
Louisville, KY

Shotput, Javelin, and Discus

Attractive you are found
Perhaps too much
So, that I have been pondering around
Gift-giving and the thoughts of such.
I'll give to you myself
A gem of sorts
As if with bug in ear from Christmas elf.
I have also gone out for sports.
The favor you'll return
And that right soon.
I cannot think of me yourself to spurn
Although for quite some time I'd moon.
I'll call you glamorous girl
As in the midst
Of party-goers with their heads a swirl
And doing all that thou me bidst.
Cheerleader you are not,
But that's okay.
I ponder and I tender parting shot
Release the joy, come as what may.

Gordon Mayfield
Lebanon, PA

I Forgot to Remember

Can my memory be on vacation
or early retirement?
I hope it's just for a limited time
that my mind has come and went.

It's a new and sad occasion
I'm experiencing all the time
But I'm sure that I'll pull through this
Now what was that on my mind?

Florence Ross
Chicago, IL

I am seventy-nine years old and the last member from a family of six. I was inspired to write this poem because of my constant forgetfulness which has become a routine part of my behavior. My parents wrote religious songs and poetry. I have written poetry since I was fifteen years old. I find it very relaxing and enjoyable. It also increases my vocabulary by looking up words in the dictionary.

The Stages Of a Relationship

All is well.
Until we meet.
Angry emotions.
No communications.
Distance.
Bedtime. Up. Work.
All is well.

All is well.
Until we meet.
Love is in the air
Sweet communications.
Bonding. Closeness.
Love is in the air.
All is well.

All is well.
Until we meet.
Face to face.
Limited communications.
Each taken for granted.
The cycle begins again.
All is well.

Debra B. Brandt
Ormond Beach, FL

My Special Dog

My dog before you was with me for seven years
When she left me I was all but in tears
She came for Bark River, Michigan ironically enough
She wasn't very smart but she was very tough
She was my child when I had none; she was my companion when men
left me with none
She never lied, she never stole; she had some choppers that were as hard
as stone
She tore the furniture more than once; she protected me from assault and
with a pounce
I grieved and suffered though you went on
My vet offered me his Pedigree and his backyard for your resting home
I only wanted you back in my arms
Shortly after you passed I ran into someone very wise;
He told me that if I could love you this much how much I could love a
human
Well I was never financially well enough to adopt a human
But, someday, I might, I will and know where I'll go
To get my child, not to Bark River, Michigan but to Nebraska
I'll get someone who will love dogs just as much as I do
In the meantime, I got another pup
She likes to run and sometimes drink from a cup
She's spoiled like you but recently I couldn't keep her
An old man who lost his wife, and somehow misses her now;
He has been taking care of my new pup the last couple of years
I was sleeping in my car and drowning in my tears.

Jerry Staley
Lorton, VA

I am a middle aged man who's been married to the same woman for over ten years. I come from a very diverse family. When I met my wife she had a dog that she had for seventeen years. It was a yellow lab mix and she loved it like the child she never had. I also loved the dog and we took it everywhere we went. We went to obedience school and somehow the dog just let us forget all about any problems the world was facing. This dog slept on our bed and ate at a special place at our dining room table.

213

Nature's Law in the Ross Creek Valley of Los Gatos

Late one crisp, dark night last fall a great big carnivore came to call.
A wild cougar out of the wood paid a visit to our neighborhood.
His quest was the most beautiful buck we had seen in many a year.
After the lion made his kill he went back to the forest
after eating his fill.
Then foxes and coyotes got their share for after the lion ate,
there was much to spare.
I told the folks of the street this is nature's way; there is nothing to fear.
After only two days and nights went by more than forty vultures filled
the sky.
How they tell the food is there I don't know, but when it happens they
never fail to show.
Those graceful and useful birds cleaned up that carcass in a very short
while.
Upon closer inspection in about a week I found that this feast other
critters did seek.
Bluejays, crows, and other birds of a feather just about cleaned it up
altogether.
A week later, with close inspection, I found only ants cleaning up in their
style.
But this isn't the end of that natural meal for with scope you see bacteria
feeding with zeal.
While they feed at the bottom where the litter does not fall, they may be
the strongest animals of all.
A week later when I passed this spot there were just a few dry bones
scattered.
Eons ago humans would have joined in this feast but now we don't have
an appetite for the beast.
Just because we didn't join the hungry throng doesn't mean in the least
that it was wrong.
Please don't feel so much fear of this that you think nature's law should
be shattered.

Edwin D. Sayre
Los Gatos, CA

214

Frienemies

Oh, the things she tells me.
But even more intriguing are the things she holds back.
The secrets, the lies, the seemingly harmless and playful banter.
Her own dear friend, to whom she gives everything.
Yet the give-and-take seems to be one way lately,
And she realizes that it's not just lately,
But always.
She tells me she is merely a t-shirt in her closet, Replaceable.
The Pluto of her solar system,
Dispensable.
And the sad thing is,
She is right.
Her obsequious nature isn't helping matters either.
As she feels her own will being slowly stripped away,
Used in a sick plot that she wants no part of,
She thinks to herself "It will get better."
She knows it will be hard, painfully so.
And even as she tries to pull back,
To keep her will,
She experiences a loss she did not anticipate, nor welcome.
The loss of a friend.

Maddie Mitchell
Indianapolis, IN

Kitchen Wisdom

Lettuce Romaine friends
Endive into our day
Butter not forget to Leaf
Some laughter along the way
O'Kale??

Darlene Jenkins
Ivanhoe, CA

Untitled

So long it has been
all these years
Some with laughs
some with tears

Two children later
they are wonderful joys
Now almost grown
we have much less noise

What will we do
when they are both out
Will our love last?
I say, without a doubt!

Karen Albert
Charlottesville, VA

Untitled

A mom and dad
Who love you
Is very special and true.
But for us kids
Who have just one
You are special, too.

Joan Martin
Cincinnati, OH

Freedom Isn't Free

Freedom isn't what you think.
Many lives are in the brink
to keep us free and safe and sound
which allows us to parade around
and say whatever we want to say,
to blaspheme others and their ways.
Men and women give their lives,
lose their children, husbands and wives
just so we have the right to say
and think and do as we please each day.
So as you lay down your head just right,
give a thought to those who fight
to keep us free and safe tonight.

Summer Z. Hill
Lorain, OH

Ode to Be Fishin'

Oh to be fishin'
That is
What I'm wishin'
Baitin' my hook
Waitin'
On that elusive brook
Instead
I'm stuck at work
With a bunch of
Jerks

Joseph S. Mikolajczyk
Swedesburg, PA

Today's Troubled Teen

Who was I then? Please tell me when,
the future is hard enough to endure,
So I really can't say about any yesterdays,
to me they don't matter anymore.
Who am I now? I really don't know,
I'm a struggling teenager trying to grow,
I keep looking for wisdom and life's meaning
to it all, and silently pray, that the answers
come someday, and hope I will be worthy
of the call.

Vincent Collura, Jr.
Port Richey, FL

218

Baby Dear

When we heard that you were coming
To join our family tree
It really didn't matter
If you'd be a he or she

We only knew that one day soon
We'd hold you in our arms
To cherish and to love you
And melt from all your charms

So welcome darling grandchild
You're the first we've ever had
All the love we have to give
Will go to you, your mom, and dad

Rose Altman
Brooklyn, NY

The One, the Only Tish

There is a young lady
A very cute miss,
Who has a large smile
My eyes can't resist.

While the hairs on her head
Are sometimes amiss,
The twinkle in her eyes
Can fill you with bliss.

She may look thin
That isn't her wish,
But still a perfect ten—
p'iece de r'estistance dish,
This French non-cher beauty—
mademoiselle, Tish.

Dennis Petilli
Smithtown, NY

Beyond the Cocoon

To rise from the stillness
To shed the empty shell
To unfold wings of beauty
And ride the wind to eternity.

There my wings will set me down
There I'll find my quiet place
There I'll live in peace forever
In the essence of God's grace.

Gentle winds bring wings of beauty
Into the quiet of this room
Those I loved, my earthly pleasure
Meet now
Beyond the cocoon.

Patricia Ritz
Danielsville, PA

The Day I Had a Stroke

Last night I went to sleep
I didn't even have to count sheep
I woke up the next morning with a scream
I thought it was just a dream
I couldn't talk
I couldn't walk
I started to pray
Please Lord help me to say
Thank you to those who love me
Thank you that I can still see
I looked out the hospital window and saw the sun shining
The nurse said, "Oh no it's raining"
I said, "Oh no I can see the sunlight"
Everything looks so bright
My heart was still beating
So if you love me tell me today
Tomorrow I may not be able to say
I love you too
This is oh so true

Albertine Self
Brooklyn, NY

Forever

Fearing the pages of what's to come,
My mind is on the run.
Miles of things to see,
Not much room to breathe.
Make my way to the start,
Myself is torn apart.
Stops my hopes,
Stops my plans.
Now maybe I understand.
I want to see all the action
Folding inside within.
Reactions fly inside,
Wondering should I hide?
Make room for my time
Because all is yet to come.
Please, please
Make it my turn,
My turn
To see what is yet to come.

Edwin R. Newmans
Winder, GA

Every Day Is Thanksgiving

Even though I clutch my blanket and growl when the alarm rings each morning, thank you, Lord, that I can hear. There are those who are deaf.

Even though I keep my eyes tightly closed against the morning light as long as possible, thank you, Lord, that I can see. There are those who are blind.

Even though I huddle in my bed and put off the physical effort of rising, thank you, Lord, that I have the strength to rise. There are many who are bedfast.

Even though the first hour of my day is hectic, when socks are lost, toast is burned, tempers are short. Thank you, Lord, for my family. There are many who are lonely.

Even though our breakfast table never looks like the pictures in the magazines and the menu is at times unbalanced, thank you, Lord, for the food we have. There are many who are hungry.

Even though the routine of my job is often monotonous, thank you, Lord, for the opportunity to work. There are many who have no job.

Even though I grumble and bemoan my fate from day to day and wish my circumstances were not quite so modest, thank you, Lord, for the gift of life.

Pam Little
Resaca, GA

I am a person who loves Jesus and nature. I like to take time out to stop and smell the flowers and watch my children play. My job consists of working with children. I am a "Dukes of Hazard" fan. I enjoy singing and spending time with my husband, two daughters, son, and big family. My inspiration comes from my thanksgiving to God for his tender loving mercy. My inspiration also comes from my cousin who's deaf, my granddad who was bedridden and from people who cannot see God's creation, and people who are hungry, lonely, and have no job.

224

Promises On Paper

promises of hope and love
promises to rise above
promises of me and you
promises of only us two
promises on paper

promises meant and said
these of which I was gladly led
promises to die together
promises of us forever
promises on paper

promises broken apart
promises that crushed my heart
promises that will never be
promises that now only I see
you told me love never dies
so why am I the one who always cries?
only promises on paper

but paper rips, love does fade
and now you are gone, gone away
so where is that paper now?
away with you, the cursed vow

Lindsay Mims
Woodbine, GA

Grandson

There is a young lad who is still tall and handsome;
who is this lad you may ask, it's grandmother's grandson.

One day he started school, and the years flew by all too soon;
from grammar school, middle school, and on to high school.

Something happened, graduate he did not do;
a big disappointment to Grandmom when she heard the news.

Grandmom prayed all through his life God would keep him under his
wing, and help him to do the right thing.

Another year and a half it took before his graduation,
but Grandmom was proud and happy to offer her congratulations.

The future of this precious lad is still unknown,
what path he will take is his choice alone.

But one thing is sure, the right decision he will make,
he proved once again he has what it takes.

Congratulations again, Grandson,
for the victory you have won.

Nettie M. Rekowski
Trenton, NJ

Times Are Always Changing

Times are always changing.
Our lives rearranging.
Just knowing God is always there
Helps us get through our troubles & care.
We may wish for more than we deserve.
My heart goes out to the men & women who serve.
They put their lives on the line every day.
We need to be praying for them in every way.
We all need to get our priorities straight,
Live in God's love and not in hate.
Yes we may have trouble of our own.
Just think of being in a war feeling all alone.
Missing your loved ones and friends.
Wondering if the war will ever end.
I wish I could wipe away every family's tears.
And to take away all their fears.
This is also for all who suffered 911, those who
Worked through it and those who passed away
I send out love and prayers to you every day.

Rebecca Wright
Beech Bluff, TN

Sun Up

The sea is the image of heaven, welded by a blaze of light,
Shadows seek refuge in hiding, like secret remnants of night—
Birds begin a dawning chorus, leaving their hotel tree,
Commencing with the community singing, they rejoin their club of
glee.
And sun continues the Greeley route, too busy to commune,
Old Sol may yearn for a solar love, but it is like reaching for the moon.
A transient cloud is a highway bandit, demanding a ransom of gold,
The shady drifter, in venturesome try, leaves a ball of fire cold.
Now, evening prepares for the sleepy old sun—a pillow of clouds for
its head!
The lonesome traveler, alone in the night, returns to a cold water-bed.
But moon stands lonely in the dark, when Sunshine takes its dips,
The lunar lady, with reflective glow, still longs for total eclipse!

Lester Rutsky
Brooklyn, NY

Sunset

Gradually it fades, that flaming globe
Blazing on peaks and balanced rocks
Corralling cactus-covered walls
Brilliant colors dominating the sky
Through windows in the sandstone
Sun peaks out for one last look
While we bid our fond farewell.

Clare Baker-Dukett
Tucson, AZ

What Do I Hear

Whistling of the trees
Blown by the wind or the spirit
Airplane soaring high above
Is he alone or with a friend
Look up to the top what do I see
The leaves are moving
But none have come down
Now it is quiet, what do I feel
Peace
Is he with me
I touch the tree, I feel the warmth
He is with me, and always will be

Susan Willis
West Milton, OH

Survive

Many nights I find it's hard to sleep.
The jobless rate is so high and we're in too deep.
Elderly people are barely able to pay their bills.
Traveling from church to church to make their next meal.
Christmas is supposed to be special for the children of this world.
And it's hard when you don't have toys and food for little boys and girls.
You can't afford to get sick because you don't have insurance at all.
So you go to work under many circumstances with your back to the wall.
Our teenagers run the street trying to make a fast buck.
But they wind up dead or incarcerated without any luck.
The automotive industry is bone dry.
And we all know the reasons why.
I pray to god every night keep me alive.
I want to survive.

Alona Lockridge
Detroit, MI

My World

Sitting on the ground against a big tree
Feeling the rays of sunshine on my face
Watching the wildlife scampering so free
Thinking that this is a wonderful place
The colorful leaves fall down to the ground
While the whispering wind swings the fine limbs
I'm in a world where I will not be found
As the nightfall comes light starts to dim
Now I'm in the truck headed towards my home
Realizing this day's end will soon be near
Thinking about the animals that roam
I'd rather be in the woods like the deer
When sleeping I think about tomorrow
Because in the woods I'll have no sorrow

Jarod Grafton

Bedtime

Fingers of darkness stretching, reaching across my walls,
Huddled on my bed as the daylight flickers and nighttime falls.
Morbidness draws my eyes to the darkest blackest corners,
Wondering if the nights shadows take me will there be mourners,
Foreboding stares come from my once harmless dresser,
Feeling a horrifying dread that would surly kill someone lesser,
Shadows and unnamed demons flit across the floor,
A grotesque monster stands guard by the door,
My insides melting, slowly becoming useless jelly,
Every creak and groan churns the insides of my belly,
Fear creeps thru my brain turning it an ugly black,
Any minute the claw of a demon will surly slash my back,
Hoping desperately waiting the birth of a new day,
Until then in this horrid nightmare I must stay,
Minutes seem like hours and hours like years,
Keeping my eyes down avoiding menacing leers,
My hope is waning, seeping out bit by bit,
Moving just feeds my engorged fear so here I sit,
I gasp as I see light behind my curtain,
Can it be morning already, can I be certain,
Do I dare hope that this torture is ending,
Light crawls in, the shadows writhing and bending,
I grin in triumph to have survived the night,
Feeling so light and Joyous I almost take flight.

Sierra Rogers
North Vernon, IN

So Much

So much, Lord, you've given to us
So much love and prosperity,
Help us Lord thy love to see
And share this love with humanity.

So much, Lord, you've given to us,
So much bread, and milk, and meat,
Help us Lord thy care to see
And share this bread with those in need.

So much, Lord, you've given to us,
So much wood and brick and stone,
Help us, Lord, thy care to see
And share this wealth with everyone.

So much, Lord, you've given to us,
So much gladness, joy and mirth,
Help us, Lord, this love to see
And share this joy with all the earth.

Helen T. Hall
Swannanoa, NC

No Longer Am I Bound

At last! No longer am I bound by past mistakes.
I loose the cord of guilt this day and go my way with conscience clear.

What's done is done—forgiven—as each new day makes
The stepping stones of hope and faith to bridge the stumbling blocks
          of doubt and fear.

And so, I face each new tomorrow, unafraid.
A child once more; I learn to take my Father's hand and call His name.

A simple prayer, perhaps? How long since I have prayed?
Yet all I ask is that I may accept the good that now is mine to claim.

In Silence now, I let the inner turmoils cease.
Content that God and I are one in all I think and say and do.
This Union permeates my mind with perfect peace;
And for the good of all concerned—I now forgive myself and start
          Anew.

My mind is clear! My eyes alert! My heart is free!
So let the wise or foolish deeds of yesterday be damned or crowned!

I shed the cross of guilt that warped the soul in me;
And through His understanding love, I go in peace;
AT LAST! NO LONGER AM I BOUND!

Al Garvey
Phoenix, AZ

The Chair

We smiled with sheer glee,
The chair had arrived,
And we could actually see it;
The much awaited chair,
Which we were reluctant to share,
After fastidiously searching the world over.

Now at last, dare I say lair?
Majestic, in our room, sat the chair,
And it had an attractive air
About it.
The colors galore match the floor and the door,
And everything else sitting in it.
We just hope it fits, and comfortably sits,
The one destined to sit in it.

So the question that burns,
The answer we yearn,
Is whether he'll happily get in it;
So the purchase we dared,
And thus welcome the chair,
At a risk beyond explanation.
We can't wait to glean,
What Kitty will gleam:
Will the chair meet his expectation?

David W. Fry
Augusta, GA

235

Requiem For 15 Years

The ceremonies have ended and the mourners all gone home,
Your week in the community spotlight, like you, has passed.
The words have all been spoken, the tears all quietly shed,
While you lie here forever in a field of mown grass.
Most that were lost in the sadness are now slowly beginning to heal,
The funeral and the public grieving have done their part.
For friends, teachers, and well meaning neighbors, it's back to school
    and work,
So ordinary things can again go on as the clock of life restarts.
But please forgive me if I am not yet ready,
For I am still leaking pieces of my soul.
Out of the sadness for your parent's shattered hearts,
And for a family who will never be whole.
Your face, though no longer quite your own, will never more be seen,
Pictures, movies, and memories are hollow replacements for your
    earthly flesh.
No more can your mother hold you, even as still as you now might be,
For the closing of the lid is final and will remain that way as you rest.
My son was concerned that your new home should have a nice view,
And we promised to come back soon to visit,
So I'm glad to tell you that you do,
I see hills, trees, a vase, and flowers to fill it.
It is good that teenage hearts are so resilient.
As they should be focused on young love and Homecoming formals,
But I will think of you and grieve you at least one more day,
Because the death of one so young should never become my new
    normal.

Karen F. Russ
Manassas, VA

To Sharon

Today, I walk down the isle
My daughter by my side
To wed a man whom she loves
With honor and with pride

My heart is overflowing
But my eyes are filled with tears
Cause I know that she is leaving
After all these many years

Today, I share with someone else
And feel my heart grow light
To hope that you will walk though life
With not a cloud in sight

There is one thing I want to say
Trust in God from day to day
When troubles start and things go wrong
Pray to him, it will make you strong

There is no smooth or easy way
That you will walk from day to day
And in the end, you will find
That God's been with you all the time

Carl H. Peterson
Grasston, MN

A New Day

In the crisp frosty morning I gazed to the east
And stared at the mountain's skyline
The light was faint but there was a reddish glow
So sunrise wasn't far behind

Tho' the morning was cold and frosty
And I could see my breath in the air
I felt awe at the Creator's power
While in reverence I continued to stare

The beauty of God's creation
Is something wonderful to behold
And I'm reminded of our elders
Of the stories they tell of old

Of times when work was much harder
And the day was dawn to setting sun
When they left fields in fading light
As their daily toils were done

When I hear these stories
Of life in the yester year
I feel safe and begin each day
With no doubts and with no fear

And as I observe the beauty
Of the beginning of another day
I give thanks as I realize
Life was not always this way

Wes Selman
Silver City, NM

I was born five miles east of Rush Springs, OK in 1928. My family moved to New Mexico in 1936. In 1946 I enlisted into the U.S Army Air Corps. After being honorably discharged in March 1949, I obtained my G.E.D. certificate and entered Western New Mexico University. I married Billie Jane McDonald in August 1950. In May 1956 I entered the U.S. Border Patrol and served twenty-seven years in the U.S. Immigration and Naturalization Service, retiring in January 1984. In 1990 I began writing poetry and I started writing a western novel.

Bloom

Life is such a mystery
And we take too much for granted.
One never knows how much time we have
And we forget to "Bloom Where We Are Planted".

We forget our loved ones are just loaned to us
And can be called "Home" anytime of night or day.
We forget to say "I'm sorry" and "I love you"
Why do we not listen and do things a different way?

When we loose a loved one, there are regrets.
Why didn't we do the things we "intended"?
Listen to your inner voice, do good things
And soon you'll automatically "Bloom Where You Are Planted."

Shirley L. TenHagen
Cape Carteret, NC

What does Barack Obama's Election Mean to You?

Has change really come to America? – Only time will tell.
Not necessarily by our leaders, but all of us as well.
The Icon is in place; however, it will take so much more,
For it is by our actions as citizens we will sink or soar!

If all our elected leaders will put solutions ahead of politics,
And our business leaders remove personal greed from the mix.
If our foreign policy is changed from handouts and a gun,
Just maybe the rest of the world would see change has begun.

Our churches seemed to have lost their purpose in life,
To take care of the basic needs and help eliminate strife.
Recycling is a way all of us can become involved,
Giving scientist the time to get the issue resolved.

America has elected a president, who happens to be black,
Think about it though, he's also half white and that's a fact!
Much of the world believes this is a wonderful thing,
I'm so proud, just the thought makes me want to sing!

It's really the American dream that opens the door for all,
Our Indians, our blacks, Hispanics and whites can stand tall.
It's not your color, religion or hereditary that will keep you behind,
But your lack of preparation, education and desire you will find.

If the Left, Right and the news media will just hang tight,
The world including us will win this fight!

Lou Mezie
Sebring, FL

That Special Day

There's one special day,
And it comes every year.
Everyone is in a good mood,
they have that magical cheer.

It's Christmas Day,
that's the wonderful dat.
People gather with presents,
And gifts, isn't that great.

They deck the halls,
with decorations and holly.
All this for Santa,
they say he's so jolly.

I met Santa once,
in a suit of red, and a beard so white.
Always so nice,
And so polite.

You'll meet him one night,
down your chimney he'll be.
Putting present after present,
under your Christmas Tree.

Chris L. Gall
Garrett, IN

Within

The eyes hold a story,
The lips give it life.
What one speaks
The mind can choose;
But what one feels,
The heart decides.

Esther Woods
Coconut Creek, FL

Touched

We walked along talking of a seasons change thru leaves of golden
brown.
Just as the wind, my arm touched a man.
My thoughts stood still.
My client kept walking.
So must I.
For the beauty of today.
For colors of red and green and golden brown.
For caregivers who cannot stop to feel a touch of wind only the beauty
of each day is theirs.
Being with their clients.

Poet Whalen
Roswell, NM

Mud

I see it now!
His plan!
I learned it from
My artist palette.

When I mixed all
My colors together
They made mud!

That the Lord did,
So that when we stick
A flower, tree, or
Shrub into it,

They bring back out
Of the mud,
The colors of the
Rainbow!

Mary Ann Carrico Mitchell, R.N.
Campbellsburg, KY

Find Help

For domestic abuse
There is no excuse
Even if you are pained
From anger or strain

There is no good reason
For rantin' and ravin'
At those who love you
And need you the most

If you think you might slip
Or lose your grip
Get some help right away
Never delay!

Don't let pride or fear
Whisper in your ear
"It's okay for today
This awful behavior

Tomorrow I'll be nicer
Yes, kinder and gentler
To those who share their lives
With me."

There will be great sorrow
When you realize
You've scarred the tomorrows
Of those you've abused today

Ted W. Johnson
Salem, OR

I was born and raised in the Willamette Valley in Western Oregon. I am the youngest of four children raised in a loving home. It was a deeply religious Christian family. I still live in Western Oregon (Salem) with my wonderful wife. We have three grown children whom we talk to frequently by phone or email. I work for the Oregon Department of Human Services. We were celebrating "Say No to Domestic Violence" month in October 2008. After hearing several disturbing stories of domestic violence in Oregon, I was moved to write my poem urging abusers to get help.

Lunch

Monkey pushes stick
Into termite hole
Pulls out stick
And eats them whole
Wonder if the monkey
Has distress
With all the creepy crawliness
Or does he have a proper lunch
By giving each of them a crunch

Morton Gold
Carlsbad, CA

Life's Treasure

Leaves bud, snow falls, eggshells of time unfolds,
Every day is cherished as a new moment of time,
a new adventure and treasure. Life, time unfolding.

Many have fallen, some have froze, eggshells are fragile,
which makes up our own.

Leaves bud, snow falls, eggshells of time unfold.

Cynthia Plympton
Gambrills, MD

Mooning

If I ever want to bare,
So folks can see my derriere;
I think that I will check my brain,
To see how much went down the drain.

H. D. Peet
Peoria, AZ

This Is Not a Dream

I wake up in the morning to this empty bed
I glance at your pillow where you used to lay your head
I can't believe it's empty now you're gone without a trace
For forty-seven years I woke up and saw your face
My heart sinks, I stare again and now I know it's true
I must start another day "alone" without you
I close my eyes and start to pray for God to ease my pain
In minutes I feel his grace and good memories
start entering my brain
I think of you and all we had the love, the kids, the fun
And know that I'll be with you "again" when at last my work is done!
Thanks be to God!

Dorothy Christensen
Nesconset, NY

Index Of Poets

LaVergne, TN USA
05 March 2010
175116LV00001B/208/P